University of the World

Dieter Lenzen

University of the World

A Case for a World University System

Dieter Lenzen
Hamburg
Germany

Springer is a brand of Springer International Publishing

ISBN 978-3-319-13454-3   ISBN 978-3-319-13455-0 (eBook)
DOI 10.1007/978-3-319-13455-0

Library of Congress Control Number: 2014955685

Springer Cham New York Dordrecht London
© Springer International Publishing Switzerland 2015
This work is subject to copyright. All rights are reserved by the Publisher, whether the whole or part of the material is concerned, specifically the rights of translation, reprinting, reuse of illustrations, recitation, broadcasting, reproduction on microfilms or in any other physical way, and transmission or information storage and retrieval, electronic adaptation, computer software, or by similar or dissimilar methodology now known or hereafter developed.
The use of general descriptive names, registered names, trademarks, service marks, etc. in this publication does not imply, even in the absence of a specific statement, that such names are exempt from the relevant protective laws and regulations and therefore free for general use.
The publisher, the authors and the editors are safe to assume that the advice and information in this book are believed to be true and accurate at the date of publication. Neither the publisher nor the authors or the editors give a warranty, express or implied, with respect to the material contained herein or for any errors or omissions that may have been made.

Printed on acid-free paper

Springer is part of Springer Science+Business Media (www.springer.com)

Contents

1 **Three Ideas of the University in the Globalization Process** 1
   References 9

2 **The Dynamics of Global Social Systems** 11
   2.1   The Dynamics of Global Social Systems 11
   References 14

3 **Global Challenges in the Post-Secondary Sector as a Springboard for Comparing Systems** 15
   References 18

4 **On the Genesis of Three Distinct University Systems in the Post-Secondary Sector** 19
   Reference 21

5 **Convergence and Divergence: Current System Dynamics in the Post-Secondary Sector** 23
   5.1   Theory of the University 23
   5.2   The Idea of Education 25
   5.3   University Admission 28
   5.4   University Autonomy and Academic Freedom 30
   5.5   Differentiation in the Postsecondary System 32
   5.6   University Funding 34
   5.7   Individual Dynamics of the Three Post-Secondary Systems 37
   References 39

6 **Fair Chances in a World University System?** 41
   References 45

7 **Conclusion** 47

References 51

Chapter 1
Three Ideas of the University in the Globalization Process

What will the university and institutions of higher education throughout the world look like in 10 or 20 years? Will they be vocational institutions based upon the most common, that is, utilitarian Anglo-American, model? If so, will they be open to entire single generations? Or will they promote top research designed to supply the industrial sector with new product ideas, innovations, and top personnel, making them institutions for a small elite? Is there a chance that the world's universities may (once again) become authentic educational institutions with the express purpose of forming individual personality, of cultivating citizens of the world prepared to assume social responsibility? Will these be limited to an educational elite, or can they serve entire generations of young people on all continents? Will, can, or should there be but one kind of university or extensive diversity in the tertiary sector, or post-secondary system? And above all, what is desirable? Which view of higher education will best serve the future of humankind in a unified world? What can we expect if (as yet) very different systems begin to resemble one another? Which model will prove dominant? Who will profit and who will not? What would need to be done to prevent a (perhaps not entirely) arbitrary dynamic from leading the utilitarians to victory in a global university system?

The German university system and continental European post-secondary education are facing fundamental transformation, a process which has to some extent already begun. It was initiated by phenomena such as the Bologna Process, a reform of European universities which seemed at first to result from an exclusively European bid for unity in higher education but which must be seen as part of globalization in the entire post-secondary system in various regions of the world. By adapting certain aspects of the Anglo-American higher education system, the Bologna Process as a fundamental reform of the European university system extends well beyond Europe. It induces continental Europe to espouse views of the tertiary sector which have already gained a foothold in North America, parts of Asia, and even in some of the emerging countries of other continents.

This process may be interpreted as part and parcel of an arbitrary (or deliberate?) process of convergence to which other phenomena have also contributed. These include student mobility between European and non-European countries, which has increased by 10% in the last 10 years[1]; numerous university partnerships, 20,000 of which are maintained to varying degrees by German universities; and the emergence of post-secondary joint NGOs such as the European University Association (EUA) or, beyond Europe, the International Association of Universities (IAU) and the International Association of University Presidents (IAUP).

This process of globalization is happening at a rapid pace, without the benefit of international oversight by democratically legitimated organizations. In fact, post-secondary education is essentially governed by a view of education as a commodity. Presumably, this process will accelerate so much in the next one to two decades that educational systems based on other traditions will virtually disappear. These traditions include the East Asian understanding of education and, of particular relevance to Germany, the continental European understanding of education.

Since the end of the eighteenth century, continental European universities have regarded themselves as institutions of enlightenment, not as institutions of vocational training or contract research. As institutions of enlightenment, universities in continental Europe, and especially in Germany (although in France, as well), have traditionally felt a two-fold commitment to the individual and to society. They serve individuals by providing them with an academic education and they thereby serve the society which these individuals guide on its path towards humanization.

The difference to the Anglo-American understanding of higher education becomes especially clear when we consider *Some Thoughts Concerning Education* by John Locke, one of the fathers of the Atlantic educational idea and a man who saw the education of a gentleman as consisting in four qualities: virtue, wisdom, breeding, and knowledge (Locke 1897). A person educated according to these precepts behaves in a manner befitting his rank and is to that extent useful. Wilhelm von Humboldt proposed a contrasting view of education is his Theory of Bildung:

> [T]he ultimate task of our existence is to give the fullest possible content to the concept of humanity in our own person […] through the impact of actions in our own lives. [This task] can only be implemented through the links established between ourselves as individuals and the world around us. (Humboldt 2010, p. 58)

Those who make decisions in the future about post-secondary education the world over must consider, on behalf of those they represent, nothing less than whether higher education institutions should serve the moral, political, and social development of society, by which I mean world society, or whether their primary task is to professionally qualify young people so that these are economically productive. Put bluntly, this is about the relationship between the economic and moral reproduction of the learning subject.

A decision either way has far-reaching consequences for the future of society the world over, for a society based on the continental European understanding pursues a utopian notion of the good, that is, not of the affluent but of the moral life,

---

[1] Unesco Institute of Statistics: Increase in the number of "inbound mobile students from non-EU countries" from 58.2% (2000) to 68% (2010).

whereas the Atlantic worldview may often value income. The conditions for and consequences of this difference extend into almost every area of society, beyond educational systems, and lead to entirely different constitutions and state practices, such as the state's use of information and its citizens' right to self-determination.

Should the university view the common good as something beyond a society's economic growth to emphasize its ethical development—even, perhaps, over and above economic considerations? This would validate what France, at the beginning of the Bologna Process, proposed as a university's duty:

> The university should thus also be the place in which nothing is beyond question, not even the current and determined figure of democracy, and not even the traditional idea of critique, meaning theoretical critique, and not even the authority of the "question", of thinking as questioning.... the principal right to say everything, whether it be under the heading of fiction and the experimentation of knowledge, and the right to say it publicly, to publish it. This reference to the public space will remain the link that affiliates the new Humanities to the Age of Enlightenment. (Derrida 2001, p. 26)

If the globalization process in the post-secondary sector, with the opportunities and risks this process entails, is not simply to be left to the workings of the market, then we must investigate the convergences which we can reasonably expect to develop naturally, as it were, without intervention from democratically legitimated organizations. This means looking at the inherent qualities and dynamics of the three great educational systems—the continental European, the Atlantic, and the East-Asian—in terms of the way they address the global challenges confronting them. Which of these systems might be best equipped to meet these challenges? Is the strongest system, with all that implies, something which the world's citizens want? If not, what can withstand such unbridled development? This will entail both resistance and dialog.

First, we need to gain a sense of the tertiary sector's development and of its universities with regard to convergences and divergences. The "tertiary sector" refers here to the entire spectrum of post-secondary training and education. This is necessary because, internationally—in contrast to Germany—the higher education sector does not distinguish between vocational training and university education; both are viewed as post-secondary education. Germany, on the other hand, is unique in offering vocational training outside the university in a so-called "dual system," which involves educational training provided by public educational institutions and part-time professional training, or full-time professional training by public institutions for so-called assistant professions. This fact is easily overlooked in the benchmarking processes used in Germany as well as in the forging of policy within the context of the Bologna Process. This has led, particularly in the latter case, to grave distortions. The Bologna Process' one-sided focus on vocational training can be explained only if we take into account that Great Britain's educational system, and the world shaped by that system's principles, sees vocational training as a university's primary task.

The views elaborated here are based on the German post-secondary sector so that, from Germany's unique position, we can consider the implications of a completely divergent understanding of the tertiary sector in the rest of the world for the future of German higher education. This analysis is important because there have been significant changes in Germany's higher education system resulting in part from German universities' attempts at adapting to convergences in the international university system—attempts which have created differences within the German university system itself which are not traditionally inherent to this system and which only arise when German university institutions try to conform to the international university landscape.

Another peculiarity, which does not apply to the university system the world over, plays a major role in this development: the principle which dictates that German universities are not only obligated to provide (vocational) training—in other words, to teach—but to make research an integral part of a university's profile. This view has expanded in the last several years to universities of applied science. Internationally, however, research universities are not the norm, they are the exception. This can be seen, for example, in the United States, where there are roughly 4,800 universities or colleges for just 100 research universities.

Due to the special significance of vocational training in international higher education systems, moreover, countries in transitional phases are undergoing extreme massification in their higher education programs. This is also due to the fact that, outside the university, career prospects—even for handworkers—are dim. Of course, those countries that have always had classical educational systems have also been experiencing an enormous increase in students, most recently in German-speaking countries, with an almost 50% increase in young people with a higher education entry qualification. These were preceded in Europe by British universities, which experienced a student increase from 500,000 to 2.4 million between 1980 and 2008. It is estimated that in countries such as India and Malaysia, the numbers of students doubled or even quadrupled between 2003 and 2008. As for China, student rates almost quintupled and UNESCO estimates that, in the higher education sector alone, there was an increase world-wide from 13 million in 1960 to 150 million in 2008 (Foskett and Maringe 2010, p. 307). If we consider these developments from the inception of the modern university at the beginning of the nineteenth century, both throughout the world and in different regions of the world, we can observe an erratic increase since the 1980s (Figs. 1.1 and 1.2).

In this respect, the German university system is also part of the globalization process and to a certain extent its victim. The understandable world-wide interest in adequate training and reasonable professional prospects has increased exponentially and has also taken hold in Germany. It did not happen, however, because Germany had no system of vocational training, as is the case in many countries of Southeast Asia; it happened because people failed to recognize that the German dual system provides vocational training of a very high standard and, due to the completely inappropriate accusations launched by the OECD with regard to participation in higher education in Germany, a significant number of single generations of students have now chosen university education. This happened on the one hand because of concern about professional prospects; on the other, no doubt, because of concerns about reputation and prestige, which are in turn very closely linked to the former. It is not hard to recognize, however, that by adapting to the Bologna system,

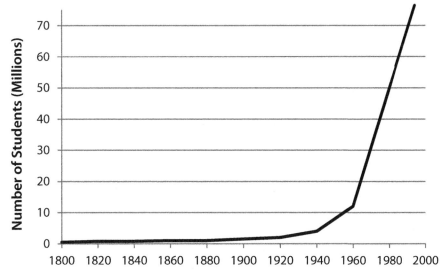

Fig. 1.1 World tertiary students, 1815–2000. (Reproduced from Meyer and Schofer 2007, p. 48)

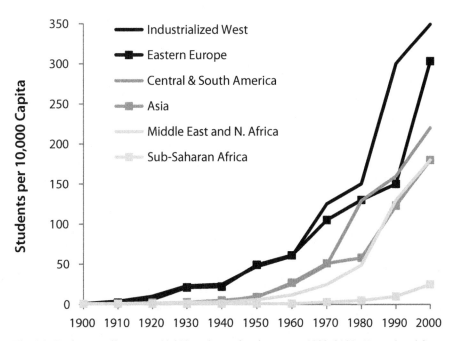

Fig. 1.2 Tertiary enrollment per 10,000 capita, regional averages 1900–2000. (Reproduced from Meyer and Schofer 2007, p. 49)

German universities largely fail to offer suitable vocational training and cannot but fail to do so because, at least within the university sector, institutions have simply transformed classic university curricula from the pre-Bologna German university system to conform to the curricula used within the Bologna system.

Against this backdrop, the question of the German university's proper place and, particularly, its curriculum, is a significant one—unless we want to utterly transform the dual system into a university system, for which there isn't any evidence. Over and beyond the question of vocational training, however, the German university's place in a world university system depends upon the nature of the university's understanding of education and how this is reflected in its curriculum. The question will naturally arise as to whether the German university system vocationalizes—to the detriment of the dual system—or whether we can succeed in strengthening the German, or more accurately, the continental European view of the university to such an extent that it might influence the emergence of a world university system. After all, the continental European view of the university, which has been significantly corrupted if not entirely sacrificed by the Bologna Process, has provided a guiding principle for modern democratic social systems and basic human rights.

To assess this development by looking at its conditions is to ask in which ways the changes in the international university system may be a part of a larger process of global change affecting all national societies.

With regard to this question, there are at least two explanations for the conditions and consequences of globalization which are not necessarily irreconcilable but do, indeed, differ with regard to the extent of potential convergence.

The first assumes significant convergence in universal questions of civil society, economic development, justice, and the administration of justice. This convergence is largely based on consensus about human rights, natural resources and—which is important in this context—education as forming personality ("Bildung") and providing professional qualifications ("Ausbildung"). John W. Meyer and others who propose this convergence model of globalization over and against that of the nation state presume that other models of the world possess little legitimacy (Meyer et al. 1997). To the extent that such a universal understanding includes notions of education in all of its manifestations ("Erziehung", "Bildung", "Ausbildung"), it would naturally have direct consequences for the emergence of a world view of the university. In the context of a rational modernity, taken moreover as a basic universal principle, any deviating concept that is not based on universal principals is seen as reactionary. To a certain extent, this shared understanding can be seen as guiding a new, almost "religious" elite represented by academics and intellectuals.

An alternative understanding of globalization takes empirical data into account. According to this understanding, we might observe a process of globalization involving, on the one hand, convergences, and, on the other, local, regional, and national processes of divergence, provided that the institutions implicated in these processes respectively filter, somehow, the uncertainty caused by globalization (Aktionsrat Bildung 2008, p. 19). This thesis was proposed at a very early stage by Norbert Elias (Elias 1969), who viewed globalization processes and concomitant regionalization as phenomena of modernity. This thesis is significant for the academic and university system because a potential university culture that is not internationally homogenous depends upon it. This is especially true for Germany, although it is also true for other German-speaking countries and, to a certain degree, for university systems in the continental European tradition (of which more below). Accordingly, Elkana and Klöpper also assume that globalization "has little influence on [elements of] local culture and society (language, art, religion, etc.) which are not directly subject to the forces of global markets, or has even nurtured these by provoking defensive reaction or the purposeful marketing of otherness." (Elkana and Klöpper 2012, p. 86) This naturally raises the question as to what extent market-free societal zones even exist or, on the contrary, to what extent societal zones might deliberately be regionalized through de-marketization in order to preserve values and norms which are deemed indispensable (for world processes, as well).

If, due to marketization, such regionalities have no chance, the first model of globalization is more likely. This may be reflected, at least in part, by developments currently characterizing most university systems: the proliferation of universities, the rapid increase in student numbers, the expanding significance of universities in society, the academization of ever more aspects of culture and society, a substantial increase in the number of professors—in short, the infiltration of societies by the university (Frank and Meyer 2007, p. 22). In light of these developments, we can assume that globalized societies will also adopt a universal view of academia. This consists in the belief that, in principle, the entire world can be perceived as a single entity, following natural laws which can essentially be understood by anybody (Frank and Meyer 2007, p. 28). Clearly, this conviction can only gain credence if it is held by the cultures from which universities and higher education institutions in various regions of the world derive their legitimacy or, to go further, their theories of education.

This raises the question as to whether there are noticeable fundamental differences in the understanding of a university's duties, goals, and procedures and to what extent such—perhaps minor—differences can be interpreted as clusters of university traditions and approaches. Presumably, this is possible and in principle, we can distinguish three traditions:

1. A continental European university tradition, which is native to Western societies and characterized by the humanistic idea of education in an academic context.
2. An Atlantic university tradition which involves a transformation of the continental European in line with pragmatic theory and, above all, as a result of fundamentally different socioeconomic starting conditions.
3. An East Asian university tradition, which—viewed historically— is about 1,000 years old and emerged from China's specific self-reproducing dynastic tradition, although it spread throughout the East Asian world and currently exercises some influence.

The legitimate question as to whether other university traditions, for example on the Indian subcontinent, in Africa, or in South America, should be taken into consideration can only be answered at the moment in the negative. Prior to colonization by the British and the emergence of the first university institutions in the nineteenth century, India did not have a comparable tertiary system and was in this respect also colonialized. However, due to extensive privatization measures in this sector, new potentially viable definitions of the university have been emerging which have not been able to make an impact in the rest of the world. As far as Africa and the Near East are concerned, it may also be assumed that, with the exception of the Islamic "universities," there was no pre-colonial tertiary system in the Arabic or Islamic African world. The still-extant Islamic concept propagated by the Al-Azhar Mosque, which was founded in 988 A.D., and other Islamic universities has, in principle, the potential to become an autonomous and, under certain conditions, influential one. At the moment, however, attempts at adapting the Atlantic view predominate. Finally, we should look at South America, particularly Brazil. Its many Roman Catholic universities, which are equally informed by religion and existed prior to and now alongside systems which have adapted the Atlantic system, also have a not entirely insignificant status. Due to the pressures of modernization hailing from the North, however, they no longer represent an autonomous university concept distinct from the three basic concepts of the university mentioned above.

Furthermore, there is a growing dichotomy between state and private institutions, the latter of which now educate roughly 75 % of all university students. We could look at still other world regions, such as the Australian system, which is also shaped by the Atlantic tradition. This would reveal the global expanse of the utilitarian-pragmatic approach to higher education.

Against the backdrop of these global developments, the question arises—particularly with regard to the future of national systems such as the German one—as to how the relationship between these three basic concepts of post-secondary education will develop. Therefore, I will begin by sketching conceivable system dynamics. Second, I will establish categories for comparing systems. Third, I will compare these systems in their present manifestations. Fourth, I will make a prognosis of likely developments should there be no organized intervention on a global scale; this analysis is based on an impression of the challenges facing all university systems. Fifth, I will explore the question as to what extent natural system dynamics can even be influenced and by what measures. Finally, I will sketch the skeleton of a world university which would need to meet the standards of a university ethics.

References

Aktionsrat Bildung. (2008). Bildungsrisiken und – chancen im Globalisierungsprozess. Jahresgutachten 2008 des Aktionsrat Bildung. Published by vbw – Vereinigung der Bayerischen Wirtschaft e.V., Wiesbaden.
Derrida, J. (2001). The Future of the Profession or the University Without Condition. In T. Cohen (Ed.), *Jacques Derrida and the Humanities. A Critical reader* (pp. 24–57). Cambridge: Cambridge University Press.
Elias, N. (1969). *Über den Prozess der Zivilisation. Soziogenetische und psychogenetische Untersuchungen. Zweite, um eine Einleitung vermehrte Auflage. Zwei Bände*. Bern: Francke.
Elkana, Y., & Klöpper, H. (2012). *Die Universität im 21. Jahrhundert. Für eine neue Einheit von Lehre, Forschung und Gesellschaft*. Hamburg: Ed. Körber-Stiftung. (English by translator).
Foskett, N., & Maringe, F. (2010). The Internationalization of Higher Education: A Prospective View. In F. Maringe & N. Foskett (Eds.), *Globalization and Internationalization in Higher*

References

Education. Theoretical, Strategic and Management Perspectives (pp. 305–317). London: Continuum International Publishing Group.

Frank, D. J., & Meyer, J. W. (2007). Worldwide Expansion and Change in the University. In G. Krücken, A. Kosmützky, & M. Torka (Eds.), *Towards a Multiversity? Universities Between Global-trends and -National Traditions* (pp. 19–44). Bielefeld: Transcript.

Locke, J. (1897). *Gedanken über Erziehung, Translated, Notated, and With an Introduction by Ernst von Sallwürk*. Langensalza: Beyer.

Meyer, J., & Schofer, E. (2007). The University in Europe and the World: Twentieth Century Expansion. In G. Krücken et al. (Eds.), *Towards a Multiversity? Universities Between Global Trends and National Traditions* (pp. 45–62). Bielefeld: Transcript.

Meyer, J., et al. (1997). World Society and the Nation-State. *American Journal of Sociology, 103*(1), 144–181.

von Humboldt, W. (2010). Theory of Bildung, Translation by Gillian horton-krüger. In I. Westbury, S. Hopman, & K. Riquarts (Eds.), *Teaching as a Reflective Practice. The German Didaktik Tradition* (pp. 57–62). New York: Routledge.

Chapter 2
The Dynamics of Global Social Systems

2.1 The Dynamics of Global Social Systems

Systems of post-secondary education and vocational training are social systems. When they confront one another in the globalization process, the question automatically arises as to their possible dominance or coexistence. That university system which succeeds in imposing its medium of communication upon others will ultimately be dominant, whether it is a system driven by knowledge or by economics. Whichever system succeeds forces the disappearance of other, comparable systems, since these fail to distinguish themselves sufficiently to withstand the dominant forms of communication of the system striving towards dominance.

Thus, there are three conceivable courses which a world university system might take in a global competition:

1. Post-secondary educational systems or academic systems could coexist. This remains the case, and was the case, as long as the three large academic and educational systems in the tertiary sector are not or were not dependent upon communication with one another. Historically, this applied to the continental European system of personality formation through active participation in scientific research, which had not been confronted with any alternative. There was no noteworthy contact to the much older East Asian system, at least none posing a threat to stability. In contrast, around the Meji Restoration in Japan in the nineteenth century, the East-Asian system was lastingly influenced by the Prussian university model. Similarly, the continental European system dominated in the nineteenth century in several classic American universities which had adopted Humboldt's model. To that extent, we can speak of a co-existence of non-communication before the nineteenth century and of a nineteenth-century phenomenon which in some respects could have led to the collapse of non-continental European systems. This didn't happen; instead, the American university system in particular responded by intelligently distinguishing itself, creating new forms, such as liberal education, as influenced by Humboldt's ideal of general education.

2. A university system can, in a confrontation with other systems, gain worldwide dominance, subordinating the others or even forcing their disappearance.

The nineteenth-century continental European university system did not pursue any such aim. Rather, East Asian and American appropriations were the product of these systems' own efforts, and not any imperial designs on the part of continental Europe. Today, however, the case is otherwise with regard to the Atlantic system. The United States began at an early stage to practice a kind of world-wide university imperialism, among other things by establishing international "American universities." By founding these, it has tried to gain a foothold in various regions of the world. This early concept (the first international American university was founded in Cairo, Egypt in 1919) continued to be pursued following the rise of a new world order at the end of the Second World War; it is interesting, however, that this did not happen in continental Europe, whose understanding of the university, based on an almost 1,000 year-old tradition, remained stable but had difficulty competing with those countries outside of Europe committed to "The American Way." This applies most recently to Iraq, for which the country's education minister, Ali Mohammad Al-Hussein Ali Al-Adeeb, sought the founding of a second American university, following the one in Sualimani, in Baghdad, reasoning, "Students here would be broadly educated in the liberal arts and sciences, but with depth in those areas that will lead to successful careers in Iraq and the region." (Al-Adeeb 2013, p. 24f.) More recently, the United States have continued with efforts to establish the Atlantic system worldwide. For example, the American Council on Education (ACE) recently published a study entitled Strength through Global Leadership and Engagement, which is dedicated to the question of "how to save the US advantage in global higher education" and which would like to see "American higher education as a global leader." (American Council on Education 2011) The study analyzes the decreasing number of university-educated US citizens in comparison to the number of university-educated students in Asian countries and the decrease in scholarly publications between 1981 and 2009 in comparison to those in the Asia-Pacific region and the European Union. It further identifies a decrease in the number of international students in the American share of the world university market. This analysis goes hand in hand with the diverse crises Hans N. Weiler has identified in the American university landscape: a financial crisis, a crisis of competition, a political crisis (anti-intellectualism), and a crisis of meaning (Weiler 2010).

In a slightly less aggressive manner, the US Department of Education recently published, for the first time, a strategy for the education sector entitled Succeeding Globally Through International Education and Engagement (U.S. Department of Education 2012). The study leaves in no doubt that the goal is global success; it tries, however, to put benchmarking procedures and educational diplomacy in its own internationalization efforts in the foreground, among other things by strategically including international education experts. There can be no doubt that the Atlantic academic and university understanding is the very one which has become, due to geopolitical as well as expansionist processes in education, the most widespread in the last several years—if not the last one-and-half centuries (with regard to Great Britain). Even if American educational policy literature expresses patently unjustified concern about a possible loss of dominance in this area, it is clear that the Atlantic university system, through different mechanisms, already dominates to such an extent that the continental European and the East Asian systems must make extraordinary efforts to validate some of their own features on a world-wide basis. Several mechanisms are at work:

As far as continental Europe is concerned, it is clear that the Bologna Process as a fundamental university reform has been decisively influenced by the British and backed by decades of Anglo-American academic systems in places like Scandinavia or The Netherlands. The introduction of "employability" as a criterion, the conviction that the imparting of skills is the goal of university instruction, and the introduction of degrees within a three-tiered system (BA, MA, PhD) in addition to many other aspects of the Bologna Process are purely Atlantic in origin. It is only at second glance, upon implementation, that they collide with the continental European understanding of the university and academia. It remains to be seen whether these formal changes so deform classic academic curricula that these are sacrificed on the altar of utility. For utility is the real purpose of education according to Locke's pedagogical realism or Dewey's pragmatism.

By the dominance of the three-tiered university system as well as by the decades-old prevalence of engineering and the natural sciences, the East Asian understanding of education could be significantly affected (see below). It also remains to be seen whether the East Asian, Confucian commitment to social harmony, which must be the aim of any form of education, has a chance of survival.

The threat to the continental European and East Asian academic and educational traditions seems to lie in the notion of utility, which was fed and legitimated by the high degree of economization of all existential concerns following the collapse of the East-West divide. Viewed systemically, the university system—influenced by the Atlantic understanding—began to alter its code of communication: education is no longer guided by the question of whether knowledge is true or untrue; it is guided by economics and the question of whether something pays or doesn't pay. Put simply, whether or not something belongs to the dominance-striving Atlantic academic understanding is determined, not by whether an utterance is true or false, but by whether or not you can earn money from it.

3. In principle, there is only a third way out of the structural trap which arises when a university system is either excluded from the globalization process or compelled to yield to the communication rules of the market in accordance with the Atlantic model: The alternative would be to find, beyond coexistence and dominance, a common world university system which, on the one hand, relies upon consensus about basic rules for academic systems and, on the other, permits divergent interpretations and approaches which do justice to the diversity of regions, milieus, and customs. This third way would require the three large types of university and academic systems to have, if possible, a historically saturated set of beliefs or convictions and to have views of the future upon which consensus can be reached. To judge the possibility for this third way, we need to compare systems. This comparison must be based on the same categories as, for example, the understanding of academia or studying, and these categories must be fundamental in a way that, on the one hand, they are historically significant and, on the other, they are relevant

to the present and the future. These categories are relevant if they allow different responses to the challenges facing all academic and university systems.

References

Al-Adeeb, A. M. A. (28 Dec 2013). Why Baghdad Needs an American University. *The Chronicle of Higher Education*, p. 24f.

American Council on Education. (2011). "Strength Through Global Leadership and Engagement. U.S. Higher Education in the 21st Century". Report of the Blue Ribbon Panel on Global Engagement. Washington, DC.

U.S. Department of Education. (2012). Succeeding Globally Through International Education and Engagement. U.S. Department of Education International Strategy 2012-2016. Washington D.C.

Weiler, H. N. (2010). *Higher Education in Crisis. Is the American Model Becoming Obsolete?* Stanford.

Chapter 3
Global Challenges in the Post-Secondary Sector as a Springboard for Comparing Systems

The unique growth of the post-secondary sector the world over, including the increased significance of research, can essentially be attributed to the not inaccurate suggestion that economic growth and wealth have a linear relation to a society's or nation's commitment to the tertiary sector. At the same time, virtually all challenges of the present age have been developed and nourished from this suggestion:

- The phenomenon of the mass university
- The problem of quality assurance
- The need to maintain the capacity for innovation with regard to personnel, curricula and organization
- The university's responsibility for balancing teaching and research
- The problem of fair university admissions
- The importance of internationalizing teaching and research
- The problem of balancing basic and applied research
- The problem of basing tasks on economic, individual, or academic needs
- The relationship between public and private
- The relationship between autonomy and control
- The need to balance comprehensive and specialized subjects
- The relationship between education and (vocational) training
- The problem of brain drain
- The problem of maintaining a diversity of languages within academia
- The search for appropriate forms of teaching
- The survival chances of locally or regionally oriented types of universities
- The question of sustainability
- The growing significance of teaching technologies
- The problem of student mobility
- The diversity of skills and capabilities among first-semester students
- The problem of intellectual property, etc.

Upon closer examination, we see that a large number of these problems are related to greater interconnectedness between post-secondary systems and market imperatives. The classic continental European idea of the university did not have such problems; after all, it, in and of itself, was a reaction to those both Enlightened and Utilitarian expectations of education. Yet in the great industrial age at the end of the nineteenth century, the classic concept of general, humanistic education was increasingly confronted by these expectations. In Germany, however, the state did not respond to these problems by transforming universities; instead, it founded tertiary engineering schools and technical universities as institutions of applied science. At the end of the twentieth century, however, education was subject to renewed criticism in Germany, with claims that the classic educational ideal viewed the world solely as an object for study (Blankertz 1965, p. 7 ff.). These diverse problems, which arose against the backdrop of economization, can be bundled if we have recourse to the basic categories set forth by the continental European university concept. These categories are therefore useful ones for comparing systems:

1. The theory of the university

This theory moves along a continuum characterized by the answer to the question cui bono? In other words, the University serves the individual or society. The market-oriented university demands innovation research and basic research only insofar as these promise to provide a foundation for the innovations in question. For the classic university, there was a simple solution to the problem: neither/nor, meaning the University serves neither the individual nor society but rather both, by serving science and scholarship, which are the university's only purpose. It can therefore be claimed, without going into more precise detail here, that the individual and society profit from science and scholarship. Today's much-discussed quality problems with regard to personnel, teaching, and graduates do not arise; for when the passion for knowledge is the main concern, it is not necessary to worry about quality. The first category for comparison must therefore be the fundamental understanding of the university.

2. The idea of education

On the continuum between general education and vocational training, the market-oriented university tends towards vocational training and career. This was by no means the case in the classic university. On the contrary, university professors with a vocational bent were mocked as "Brotgelehrte" or scholars who teach merely to eke out a living. It was therefore clear that reproductive learning was secondary to productive learning or what is today called "learning by discovery." Learning by discovery can best be accomplished when learners take part in research or, as it were, these very discoveries. The answers to today's challenges, which are related to the standardization of curricula, the question of how international a curriculum should be, the language of instruction, and teaching methods all the way to instruction in massive open online courses (MOOCs) will depend upon the concept of education ("Bildung" or "Ausbildung") we choose.

3. University admissions

If university instruction serves general education purposes, the question as to admissions must be answered differently than it would be if we were talking about vocational institutions. University admissions therefore constitute the third category for comparing systems. This is especially crucial because demographic developments the world over vary dramatically—a decrease in birthrates in Central Europe leads to the problem of tapping talent reserves, while in systems in which attending university is the only path towards a career, the problem is not a dearth of human capital but a dearth of university institutions capable of accommodating the growing number of applicants. The admissions category therefore also marks a continuum, in this case between admission for all or for a few. Dealing with the question of university admissions further raises the question of educational fairness because it is a question about the just life, about the diversity of admission requirements, mobility, etc. The classic university found a solution for the admissions problem outside of its system: the concept of Hochschulreife, which means readiness for university study upon leaving secondary school with an Abitur, did not even give rise to the question of selection. Whoever had an Abitur could study. This model, which solved the problem of selection, was externalized. The problem was only re-internalized when institutional resources no longer sufficed and tools such as Numerus clausus (admission restrictions) were introduced in Germany or criteria such as the ability to pay were introduced in the countries of the Atlantic system.

4. University autonomy and academic freedom

If research and research-oriented learning are based on the logic of academia and not on the needs of society or the individual, then the logic of academia must be safeguarded. It is all too easy, as the founders of universities at the dawn of the nineteenth century knew, to subordinate academia to other interests, whether those of the Church in the past or of the market today. On the continuum between academic freedom and state control, the classic university introduced the idea of autonomy alongside that of academic freedom. The resolution to this potential contradiction was faith in the willingness of those who taught and those who were taught to adhere to the norm of disinterested pursuit of knowledge. It was only logical that the concept of academic self-governance arose for the German and other continental European universities.

5. Differentiation in the post-secondary system

Among today's problems throughout the world is the question as to whether the tertiary sector should be characterized by comprehensive or specialized universities with specific vocational profiles. Similarly, the concepts of local and universal types of universities stand in contrast to one another. On the continuum between a comprehensive university, a term which already constitutes a response to specialization, and a specialized university, the classic system opted for *universitas*, which means a unity of disciplines in a single institution. This difference is significant when comparing systems. It is also a function of a university's basic responsibility, whether general (humanistic) education or special vocational training.

6. Funding universities

The list of categories for comparison could be concluded at this point, if in the course of the last 200 years a challenge had not arisen which the Prussian state responded to by establishing public funding for an otherwise autonomous university system: the challenge of financing. The moment the conviction that university study creates significant advantages on the path towards employment and wealth gains credence—resulting in a massive volume of applications which needs to be dealt with—the question of financing rears its head. The view that the state should finance the education system and, consequently, the future of both society and the individual, can be found today in only a few nations. The resolution to the state-private dichotomy in the form of public funding for an otherwise self-governed university system has increasingly given way to the privatization of university systems the world over. This includes, in particular, the charging of tuition fees. Essentially, this is the Atlantic model of university education, which has enjoyed success in nations in which the state has far fewer financial resources than in Germany.

The six comparative categories are based on the fundamental elements of the classic university idea. Even superficial consideration reveals that these remain challenges for the world university system, although no attempts to resolve contradictions outside the extant dichotomies are being made. This classic university idea was constitutive for the continental European university idea, derived from the theory guiding the founding of the Berlin University of 1810. This Humboldtian theory of the university in Germany, which institutions and their faculty still largely see as regulative, is now, in the process of globalization, giving rise in the tertiary sector to an incompatibility between the continental European and the market-oriented, rather more Atlantic ideas of the university. A comparison makes it possible to describe the extent of these divergences before the question of the prospects for convergences can be addressed.

References

Blankertz, H. (1965). Problemgeschichtliche Vorbemerkungen zu den beiden Texten von Campe und Villaume. In: H. Blankertz (Hrsg.), *Bildung und Brauchbarkeit. Texte von Joachim Heinrich Campe und Peter Villaume zur Theorie utilitärer Erziehung* (pp. 7 ff.). Braunschweig: Westermann.

Chapter 4
On the Genesis of Three Distinct University Systems in the Post-Secondary Sector

While the continental European conception of the university has been characterized by the mechanisms for resolving the dichotomies between the individual and society; education and training; selectivity and openness; academic freedom and state control; and unification and differentiation within the higher education system, or for resolving the dichotomy between state and public funding, this is not the case for the Atlantic understanding.

Universities in the USA, some of which were already almost 200 years old, did indeed adapt the writings of German university classicists such as Wilhelm von Humboldt, Fichte, and Schleiermacher at the beginning of the nineteenth century and drew the organizational conclusions, but not in pure form. The American university system, which had not yet evolved to its current state, virtually filtered, *sub specie realitatis*, the continental European concept through Britain. The classic figure of reference is John Locke and not German Idealism. This means that the question of educational utility is not only not illegitimate per se, but, on the contrary, may form the starting point for justifying higher education. This is, of course, not only true for universities such as Oxford and Cambridge or for the later Ivy League in the United States, but for the large number of gradually emerging "normal universities." Thus, whereas in Germany the university entrance qualification is acquired externally, in the Gymnasium, and the University is not—at least in the first instance—a vocational institution, in the United States there is an institution between the secondary educational level, which is completed at an earlier age, and actual academic study called a "college"—which is either autonomous or part of a university and which confers a bachelor's degree; this degree can subsequently be "professionalized" so that, at a British university such as the University of Plymouth, you can could earn a Bachelor of Surf Management. Similarly, an American community college fulfils vocational duties when, for example, it confers a qualification for nursing. It cannot be overlooked, however, that at least in the USA, the college curriculum, consisting of 4 (and not, as in Germany, 3) years for a bachelor's degree, strongly emphasizes general education in the first 2 years, or familiarization with the liberal arts. After 1945, this feature became more significant, reflected in the self-appointed responsibility for providing general education.

It is often and erroneously assumed that the Atlantic understanding has been adopted in East and South East Asia. At first glance, you might draw this conclusion if you were to look only at the large share students or their parents contribute to finance university study. This view of things fails to recognize, however, that tertiary education, particularly in China, is older than in Central Europe or the USA. Between 200 B.C. and the eighteenth century, a system of academies (shuyuan) already existed in Imperial China and they supplied the imperial administration with loyal servants. In the period from 618 to 906, the larger Buddhist cloisters maintained such shuyuan, in which novices, monks, and the laity alike received instruction. In the eleventh and twelfth centuries, private and semi-private institutions, also known as shuyuan, emerged, although these were decentralized and instruction was organized in very different ways allowing for free discussion. There were, moreover, large state academies which were publicly funded and which constituted authentic centers of academic pursuit.[1] Academy study is not reserved for a privileged elite—it is meritocratic. Confucius' remark that a good student may become a civil servant has served as a kind of mission statement for the Chinese "higher education" system for more than a thousand years. It is accompanied by a highly rigorous examination system for future civil servants, who are characterized not just be loyalty but by a high degree of general and authoritative education. The goal of this education is to cultivate the "nobleperson", instructed to emulate intellectual and moral role models and part of an accomplished, enlightened leadership. The French and English found the examination system of seventeenth-century China so compelling that Europe adopted this Ming Dynasty concept for its superiority. Written exams tested a candidate's education, meaning knowledge of history and canonical works; the ability to analyze these works along specific ideological lines and to apply them to present-day problems; and the ability to adequately express oneself in literary Chinese. From its very inception, this examination system was criticized by Confucians as a test of rote learning; in contrast, the noble person is characterized by his moral qualities and right behavior.

The East Asian model of education spread throughout Japan as early as the eighth century after Christ and, soon thereafter, throughout all of East Asia, including Singapore. That extremely high tuition rates could be charged in these countries is due to the fact (especially in Japan) that higher education is not viewed as an opportunity to earn (and to spend) money but as a contribution by the individual and his or her parents to the conservation of social harmony (*wa*, prevalent in Japan, as well, since the sixth century): "Self-formation by learning is an act of filial piety, child's (*sic*) duty to his/her parents and the duty of parents to the ancestral lineage of the family." (Marginson 2011, pp. 598)

It is only through this fundamental understanding of education that a host of higher education phenomena in contemporary East Asia can be understood—for example, the oft-criticized "exam hell" required to enter choice universities, and much more. It is the key to understanding and the common position throughout all of East Asia, with, however, a significant interruption in China: After the first

---

[1] 1 This description is based on comments by Michael Friedrich.

Western-based Chinese University was founded in China in 1895, one which was still beholden to the Confucian ideal of education and which formed a starting point for both a classic Chinese and cosmopolitan institution of higher learning throughout the Republican era until 1949, Communist China broke with this tradition and, as a result of the revolution, took over the Soviet system more or less one-to-one. During the Cultural Revolution, these institutions were also completely destroyed, so that subsequently, in 1976, the question of restitution arose. Since then, Chinese reform governments have permitted, albeit in only a few aspects, the emergence of the old system while making recourse to the Atlantic university understanding so long as basic elements such as private funding are compatible. In this case, we are dealing with a partial convergence largely traceable to influence by the World Bank.

In summary, we can say that three (still) extant basic concepts of the post-secondary sector are characterized simultaneously by convergences and divergences. While the continental European understanding of education ultimately has recourse to a Platonic-Judeo-Christian tradition hailing back 2,000 years, and the East Asian understanding of education has an almost equally long history, the Atlantic understanding of education is something of a derivative of the continental European tradition. Throughout the epochal course of the twentieth century, however, with its world-wide geopolitical restructurings, this derivative has, due partly to internal dynamics and partly to an offensive policy of colonization, become extraordinarily influential. For these reasons, the continental European and the Confucian understanding of the university are now facing the question as to whether and to what extent they can preserve a cultural identity which, at least in specific categories of our systems comparison, aim for universality. A nuanced view of system differences in the six categories of the system comparison allows us to come closer to an answer.

Reference

Marginson, S. (2011). Higher Education in East Asia and Singapore: Rise of the Confucian Model. *Higher Education, 61,* 587–611.

Chapter 5
Convergence and Divergence: Current System Dynamics in the Post-Secondary Sector

5.1 Theory of the University

While the divergences between the three university systems or systems of post-secondary education as detailed in Chap. 3 have historically been substantial, they are not necessarily so now. If at all, the classic view of the university can be compared with that which is prevalent in today's research universities. These, however, comprise only a fraction of the post-secondary system. In the USA, for example, 100 out of 4,800 universities are considered research universities; in India there are only 10 out of 18,000 and in China 100 out of almost 5,000 (Altbach 2011, p. 12). This is not the case for the German system. Ideally, we may assume that all of the approximately 120 universities, with regard to the relationship between research and teaching, are both teaching and research-oriented. The Humboldtian ideal is still being perpetuated, at least according to self-descriptions, and can be observed in many subjects, with the exception of strictly vocational ones. Furthermore, institutions of applied science are increasingly laying claim to the pursuit of research. To this extent, the resolution of the relationship between the individual and society (humanistic education through science) as a means of orientation for a university tends to become ever more functional.

This is by no means the case in Europe. German universities or research universities can best be compared to the French Grandes Écoles, but not to normal universities with a teaching focus. If we consider that in Germany a significant share of especially costly basic research has been conducted outside university walls for decades, and to some extent since the beginning of the twentieth century, it becomes clear that research can be conducted as a classic university pursuit to only a limited extent. Thus, the assumption that quality naturally ensues from a passion for knowledge no longer automatically applies. For this reason, systems logic entailed an alternative method for ensuring quality. Quality assurance systems, which were originally implemented in the USA, particularly in private universities as a basis for and proof of accreditation-worthiness, have also spread to Europe, where accrediting systems have been adapted; due to massification, they are now used in

China, as well. In view of the emergence of these quality assurance systems, there is a noticeably significant convergence. These systems do not only encompass the quality of teaching but of human resources recruitment, governance procedures, and much more.

Similarly, neither the continental European nor the East Asian model claims any longer that every university must be considered excellent (as German universities could be due to their extensive research). The introduction of the "excellence" tag has, on the contrary, created the basis for substantial differentiation (compare 4.5). In addition to the outsourcing of basic research to external institutions, there has been a mirror-image externalization in the field of applied research—not solely, however, in Germany but in the East Asian world, as well: innovation centers modeled upon Silicon Valley have been established both in China and in European countries. Garching in Munich and Adlershof in Berlin are exemplary for Germany. Research, which in an academic context resolves the dichotomy between the individual and society, no longer has this function. In Germany, this mechanism poses a particular threat to universities insofar as basic research has increasingly been removed from their sphere of responsibility. And the same thing is happening with practically-oriented and applied research, which, due to its market orientation, is abandoning academia and becoming part of the economic system. Put bluntly, market-oriented innovation centers are not about science, they are about production.

To the extent that this is the case, there is a legitimization deficit: academic policy runs the risk of private citizens questioning why their tax money should finance these kinds of production infrastructures. To avoid this risk, all three university systems are moving in a similar direction: innovation centers are largely funded privately and shaped by this fact. As a consequence, the right to determine research topics also follows from the practice of (private) funding. The universities of the Atlantic system somewhat alleviate the problem of legitimization by, for example, declaring social services a fundamental part of their educational mission such that they can at least assume an indirect return on investment for the benefit of society. This is generally not the case in the continental European system. In the East Asian system, this question does not arise because the disciplined (self-) education of the younger generation constitutes per se a contribution by themselves and their parents to social harmony.

In summary, for the theory of the university, we can assume a high degree of convergence under the sign of the Atlantic system, which is characterized by the economization of research (and teaching). In this way, research loses the innocence it possessed in the classic continental European concept, according to which it derived its legitimacy from the methodological and paradigmatic logic of academia itself. This has far-reaching consequences for goals such as the sustainability of science and scholarship, since products created for the market—though they may be related to knowledge—must have, due to growth imperatives, the shortest "half-life" so that innovations can be successively placed on the market.

If there is to be a path towards a responsible world university system (compare Chap. 5), then the question will have to be addressed as to how far, alongside the convergence catalyst "market," the convergence factor "academic knowledge for its own sake" can be restored. The latter alone creates the conditions for successfully establishing and ensuring basic research, which is, in turn, the condition for applied research. To this extent, even a market-oriented research approach must nurture universities as places of pure science and not, on the contrary, destroy these with demands for applicability.

5.2 The Idea of Education

The market-based Atlantic approach as a main feature of convergence in the global university landscape could confirm the view that the task of universities, with regard to the next generation, is essentially to provide a market-oriented vocational education. It is this very view that has been the frequent target of criticism. The matter, however, is a bit more complex.

The continental European system, particularly in its German manifestation, assumes that the general formation of personality is the university's main task. The Berlin University's founders hoped that student involvement in research would form the key to the general formation of personality, namely through the medium of the scientific method. According to these founders, the student's adherence, "in solitude and freedom", to the strictures of methodical research pursuit would duly nurture personality and, to some extent, instill discipline. Thus, the knowledge-seeking scholar became the leitmotif of university education, a leitmotif based on the conviction that the formation of personality in this context would also lay the proper groundwork for plying any trade, even those outside university walls. This educational idea applied to both the individual and society. The individual, according to this educational theory, becomes cultivated, and society profits, even globally, from the individual's educational progress. For education (as self-creation in the process of acquiring knowledge!), conceived on a large scale, leads beyond the individual to the greater cultivation of humanity. This did not only mean that intellectual progress benefits all of humanity; it also meant the continuous humanization of man. The connection between individual cultivation of personality and collective human progress has remained unique to the continental European understanding of education. It is the basis for university instruction via research as well as a research approach which follows the logic of science and not an external logic of vocational training—a fact often criticized in the twentieth century, when the humanistic educational theory upon which it rested was no longer understood.

This denunciation implies, however, a kind of analog which can be found in the Atlantic concept. This view becomes clear when we consider that, generally, universities outside of Germany or outside of parts of Europe foster teaching. With the exception of research universities (see above), post-secondary educational institutions are generally vocational institutions. This is due to the fact that non-academic vocational training does not even exist in many countries or has become increasingly academic, a point which has frequently been overlooked in Germany. For many areas of the tertiary system, particularly those influenced by the Atlantic system, this means that young people between the ages of 16 and 18 leave the secondary school system either to work and to receive on-the-job training with their employer or to attend an academic institution in the tertiary sector. In those countries influenced by the Atlantic system, this often means that colleges provide undergraduate education, which, however, research universities also provide in autonomous, usually distinct undergraduate schools.

This becomes immediately clear when passing through selected countries which adhere to the three different ideas of the university prevalent throughout world. Great Britain, for example, offers training at the ISCED 5A level, known as "higher" or "further education," to people between 17 and 18, as well as tertiary education at the ISCED 5B level, which corresponds to a mid-level vocational qualification such as a technical degree, a Meister certificate, or an assistant profession (e.g., medical technician) in Germany. Incidentally, in 1992 Great Britain transformed their polytechnics, similar to German Fachhochschulen, into universities so that exclusively vocational programs could disguise themselves as level 5A programs. Similarly, vocational training in the USA takes place at college level. Students over 17 can choose among undergraduate programs at universities, junior or community colleges or, to a very limited extent, vocational technical institutions.

In the university systems influenced by the Atlantic system, this is, in various manifestations, a defining characteristic. With a low student rate of 26%, Brazil's post-secondary sector has 190 universities and an additional 131 Centros universitarios, with virtually no post-graduate programs; 2004 Facultades, smaller universities with fewer subjects; and a small number (40) of explicitly vocational Institutos federais. A similar vocational focus can be observed, for example, in post-Soviet Russia in the fact that programs in the tertiary sector are governed by the Federal Act on Higher and Postgraduate Vocational Education—that, essentially, academic and vocational education are mentioned in the same breath. A glance at Asia reveals something similar. Korea has explicitly looked to the Atlantic system, although it only admits students between 19 and 20 to the higher education sector, which exists alongside colleges in the form of industry colleges, junior colleges, pedagogical universities, and comprehensive vocational schools. This means that a significant proportion of a single generation attends an academic institution. Only training in technical skills takes place outside the academic sector.

The Atlantic influence can be seen very clearly in the Japanese university system. For example, the majority of students, or 73% of a single generation, leaving upper-level schools subsequently attends a university (daigaku), which also confers a first degree, or bachelor's, after 4 years. This is also increasingly the case in China. Since the opening of the People's Republic of China, the country has had 1,280 junior colleges operating at 5B level and an almost equally large number of universities with 4-year first-degree programs. Moreover, there are approximately 1,000 vocational schools with roughly 4.8 million students. Even though training in the skilled professions takes place in over 3,000 vocational institutions, vocational training outside academia is not especially significant. In 2007, only about 7.2% of all students in the tertiary sector received instruction in such non-academic institutions.

If, on the other hand, we look at post-secondary educational systems in the continental European tradition, matters look different: In Germany, it is a well-known fact that about 40% of a single generation still pursue non-academic vocational training. France has 2,258 institutions in the Section de techniciens supérieur (STS) over and against a mere 79 universities and 114 Instituts universitaires de technologie (IUT), in addition to further almost 2,000 higher schools for engineering, merchants, and other professions.

In summary, in large areas of the Atlantic and East Asian post-secondary system, as well as in the United States's state-funded post-secondary system, we are not, in fact, talking about an academic education comparable to that in continental Europe, especially Germany, but about more or less established forms of vocational training. This has consequences for curricula, the standardization of which needs to be greater than in the classic continental European system due to professional imperatives; it has consequences for the organization of teaching and studying which, due in part to the lower age of learners, is more scholastic than academic; and it has consequences for the selection of teaching faculty, which by German standards bears greater resemblance to secondary school teaching staff. Furthermore, this has consequences for the complexity of teaching subjects, which must be practical and application-oriented.

Meanwhile, the conceivable assumption that undergraduate education in a system influenced by the Atlantic one dispenses with general education is false. Early on—at the beginning of the twentieth century at the latest—the idea of a liberal education based on the concept of *septem artes liberales* was (re)integrated into the American system. And following the end of the second great war catastrophe of the twentieth century, rhetoric propounding responsibility for general education can be found in university writings time and again; for example, in 1945, when Harvard University declared that its educational mission was to enable every graduate to lead a "life as a responsible human being." In 2007, Harvard was still committed to implementing a New General Education Curriculum with a particular emphasis on the humanities (Kirby 2008, p. 143). It should not be overlooked, however, that this understanding of liberal education is different from that in the continental European model: whereas in Europe, general education is based on the belief that learners are capable of selection and that they can decide for themselves what to study (education is always self-education!), the concept of liberal education in undergraduate institutions is extensively canonized. This is true for both general-education subjects and individual aspects of the curriculum. The classroom in these institutions bears much greater resemblance to the classroom in the upper schools of the German Gymnasium prior to 1975. Kirby shows that the growing significance of liberal education has since taken hold in China:

> What is encouraging about Chinese higher education today is the independent understanding that the general education of China's students—in the arts and humanities as well as the sciences and social sciences—will be as important to their, and all of our, futures, as will be their specialized, professional training. (Kirby 2008, p. 144)

Chen Xin further describes how, in China, programs with a liberal education curriculum have been established, by all means in the awareness of the Confucian tradition, at universities such as Peking University or Fudan University in Shanghai. Xin shows that this concept is known as "cultural education" and involves basic knowledge in the humanities, the social sciences, the natural sciences, and art (Xin 2004, p. 5).

Presumably, due to the Confucian system's own canonical tradition, there is sufficient convergence with the Atlantic system. From the standpoint of German educational philosophy, however, ticking off canonical requirements is precisely the opposite of education conceived of as "personality formation." Adorno used the term Halbbildung ("half-education" or semi-literacy) (Adorno 1998).

Based on the current state of development among the three large university systems, we can perceive a high degree of convergence between the Atlantic and the Confucian system with regard to the ways in which they understand general education as canonized liberal education. We must assume that this understanding will gain ground if no substantial corrective is found. Incidentally, this is already happening in the spread of English academic language in non-natural science disciplines as well as, in some instances, via the concept of MOOCs, which can reach recipients of up to seven-digit "customer numbers" with a single lecture. To this extent, a warning is in order about an academic neo-colonialism in the guise of what are clearly meant to be humanitarian aims but which in fact do not allow for the formation of personalities educated through "devotion to the subject" (Schleiermacher, Horkheimer); instead, they reproduce standardized general knowledge by way of mimesis.

5.3 University Admission

In the continental European university system, the problem of fair access to university education did not arise. The number of people interested in such an education did not exceed more than 1 % of a single generation. This could have perhaps been higher under other social conditions, but because the concept of making a living did not play a fundamental role in the university's self-image, masses of applicants would still be unlikely under other social conditions. This means that university admission only becomes a problem the moment that university study promises advantages in working life. This is naturally the case if the link between the university educational system and the employment system is no longer weak but strong. Such a connection emerged, at least superficially, in the 1970s and 1980s, when it was suggested that talent reserves be tapped in the wake of the so-called "Sputnik Shock." Then there were the high birth rates for specific birth years. It was no coincidence that places for students first became limited in those subjects which promised closer links to particular professions—those, moreover, connected to the potential for higher income, such as medicine, veterinary medicine, pharmaceutical studies, business administration, etc. Clashes over admission to Egyptian studies are improbable.

The problem of fair access to a university system which has been partially transformed into a vocational system has been addressed by the three basic concepts of the post-secondary sector very differently. The extreme form is the German variant of the continental European system: due to the constitutional link between the right to choose a career and the right to choose a university, it became necessary to create a model of selection ensuring equal opportunity. In a tuition-free program, the Numerus clausus, or admission restriction, was chosen as a model for selecting the best students. This principle of selection seems, in the last few decades, to have passed constitutional muster.

In the other countries of continental Europe, although not in the Atlantic system, one would find a comparable problem. There, university access is governed by a double mechanism: selection based on aptitude tests and, to some extent, extremely high tuition fees, which in any case lead to lower numbers of applicants. This procedure also converges historically with the admissions procedures in the East Asian system: A good student, and only a good student, has a chance, which, in China, is explicitly viewed as a one-time chance. This is likewise true for Japan, with its "exam hell." For later employers, therefore, the specific degree from a distinguished university is less relevant than the fact that a job applicant succeeded in being admitted at a young age to a distinguished university—that he or she was tough enough to endure the extreme stress.

In universities of the East Asian system parents also have significant tuition fee obligations, as already shown. These do not, however, influence selection, since responsible parents and relatives are unconditionally prepared to devote their full energies for the rest of their working lives to paying off the debt created by their child's or children's studies. The debt problem, incidentally, is also faced by American graduates. There, the total debt of young people now amounts to 1,058 billion $ (as of 2012) (Michler 2013, p. 21). While there is a high degree of convergence in this instance, this is only partially the case for continental Europe. In Great Britain, universities recently raised tuition fees for academic study substantially, virtually destroying the humanities, since these do not seem to promise immediate career benefits.

Insofar as university study actually offers better (or any) opportunities on the labor market, the question of fair university access intensifies. The fact is that in China the problem of growing inequality has been noted (Henze et al. 2013, p. 59) as laborers from non-coastal and industrial regions, even with huge effort, cannot guarantee the university education which would provide a better life. The question thus arises as to whether and how long access inequality can be legitimatized by admission tests. After all, in Japan, as in other East Asian countries, this is still, astoundingly, the case, at least in the "better" universities. Education is seen as the responsibility and obligation of parents, not of society as a whole, even though society profits in the same way as the individual. This is similarly true for the Atlantic university conception. The university system in the United States, however, is in a position to offset the effects of inequality for more than 50 % of students by offering scholarships, at least for the gifted and talented.

Even if one could assume otherwise, the problem of fair access in Germany, despite the absence of tuition fees, has not been solved, since state governments are not prepared, on behalf of the federal government, to assume the costs for all applicants who have the right to study. The problem will intensify if a significant number of working men and women claim expanded rights to attend university. The expectation perhaps entertained by many politicians that the demographic downturn in Germany will solve the problem is deceptive if, at the same time, further hurdles to access fall and the (false) suggestion that university study generally offers vocational training is upheld or if, as the German manifestation of the Bologna Process would have it, the German universities are actually transformed into vocational schools. In summary it can be said that for all three university systems the question of access is being addressed intensively, if in different ways.

To sum up, let me state that with regard to university admissions, there is significant divergence from the German variant of selection: In Germany, the selection mechanism of money is (or has become) for the most part meaningless due to the abolition of tuition fees, while achievement requirements have been significantly liberalized. In contrast, the Atlantic and East Asian systems are convergent with regard, on the one hand, to money as a necessary private resource to finance study and, on the other hand, to in part extreme expectations for (previous) achievement which is evaluated in comprehensive selection procedures.

5.4 University Autonomy and Academic Freedom

Do the providers of the three basic systems of the post-secondary sector trust faculty to perform adequately and do they have faith in students' willingness to learn? Today, the answer for almost all systems is "No."

This is not very surprising for the Atlantic and East Asian systems. If, with the exception of research universities, research—meaning new insights—is not the object of university pursuit but vocational training is, then the trust-inspiring mechanism of a passion for knowledge is lost. British and American professors who teach at provincial universities or community colleges are just common employees. They do not enjoy the special social recognition that scholars in the German university system did through the 1960s. The Atlantic system does not therefore have any kind of academic self-governing system comparable to the continental European system, which ensures that employees can assert their interests. As a rule, their interests are in fact represented by unions within corporate-like institutions, just as in every other production plant. The mass university model introduced in continental Europe, especially in Germany, in the 1970s, with participatory rights for professors, academic assistants, non-academic staff, and students, has no place whatsoever. This model does not even apply to research universities. As Altbach laconically states: "Research universities cannot be democratic; they recognize the primacy of merit, and their decisions are based on a relentless pursuit of excellence." (Altbach 2011, p. 16).

The dictate of market-oriented vocational training as well as the dictate of research with the same orientation, in addition to the various interests of various groups within an institution in the tertiary sector, do not allow, from an Atlantic perspective, a democratic imperative for action. This is no different for the countries under the East Asian system or their universities. Here, however, the authority of those who teach compounds market dictates. Put simply, professors are right, and

5.4 University Autonomy and Academic Freedom

there is nothing further to discuss. This is true in both non-continental European systems, mutatis mutandis—naturally for curricular topics, as well—with programs as binding as the subjects chosen by faculty. And due to financial imperatives, this applies equally to scientists' research topics. Research funding largely derives from private and public contracts, which answers the question as to intellectual freedom. This consists at most in the ability to decide not to do research. The risk of having annually negotiable salaries downgraded, however, is high and for non-tenured professors even poses a threat to their existence. In this respect, the East Asian university landscape, particularly in its most recent Chinese manifestation, does not differ from the Atlantic's. It is characterized by full "acceptance of market-driven regulation processes." (Henze et al. 2013, p. 53).

This phenomenon is beginning to make headway in the continental European landscape, as well. While university professors up through the 1970s were still sufficiently capable of conducting research with their basic resources in a large number of disciplines, today they no longer are. At best, they can generate, on the basis of their basic resources, applications for research projects in the large, program-oriented grant processes by government ministries, foundations, and corporations, or they have to subject themselves to peer evaluation—albeit of a purely formal nature—within the selection system of the German Research Foundation, whose acceptance quota, even for applications with top evaluations, has continued to sink. In the research field, therefore, there has been a noticeable and steady decrease in freedom, especially since peers, due to their own involvement in the market-oriented mainstream of their disciplines, subconsciously tend more and more to judge according to the mainstream.

It is further obvious that individual freedom for professors and students has been significantly limited by the Bologna Process and the exhortation to vocational training. Today, a university professor does not teach primarily in his or her research area but, at best, in others' research areas or from textbooks.

The severely limited academic freedom of faculty and students is inversely proportional to an institution's degree of autonomy as a whole. To this extent, we are dealing with a double convergence: loss of freedom at the individual level, greater collective freedom for the organization. For the continental European tradition, particularly in its German manifestation, this was nothing special. The Prussian state tried as far as possible to keep out of academic pursuit while ensuring scholars' loyalty to the state by conferring civil service status. The Prussian model was derived from the East Asian one (Marginson 2011, p. 596). The gap between the State and the University was thus politically intended.

This does not necessarily apply to the Atlantic system. The critical distance to the state maintained by the American university system results from the formation of the university system as, at least in part, a private enterprise system. Because, in accordance with the American view of the economy, the state has only very limited influence over production, and universities are similarly conceived as managerial universities, there is no effective influence upon university activity. Even quality controls and subject oversight in the American system have to some extent been privatized by virtue of being outsourced to accreditation agencies. Most recently, however, under the influence of the Obama administration, there have been noticeable amendments, however small. To this degree, the first publication of a strategy for the tertiary sector by an American federal ministry is a veritable breach of taboo (US Department of Education 2012).

In the East Asian system, conditions are not uniform, owing to deviating political conditions, at least in China. Until recently, centralized micromanagement was the norm. In due course, the possibly justified fear of the emergence of a chaotic process arose, a fear not related solely to public education. Most recently, China's open-door policy seems, however, to have inspired two developments: a transition from state control to state supervision and a decentralization of responsibility to small political units in the form of provinces and regions, with, however, a penchant for micromanagement.

In summary, while there is significant convergence in all three systems with regard to limitations on individual freedom, the situation is unclear with regard to organizational autonomy. For example, there have been liberalization and decentralization efforts in East Asia, the USA, and Great Britain. In contrast to these developments, there have also been attempts at state control, to a significant degree in Great Britain as the country of origin for the Atlantic system, and in continental Europe. In many countries, there have been re-budgeting efforts, at least in those places where responsibility for university policy is assumed by political parties that tend to support state intervention, as in the Russian Federation or in a majority of German states, insofar as the latter have become social democratic. But even conservative administrations are not free from the temptation to supervise subjects in the postsecondary sector, especially with regard to its transformation into a vocational institution. This, however, owes more to the regulatory interests of ministerial civil servants than to the interests of politicians. Consequently, regulation imperatives differ among the three university systems, with participation at the heart of matters in Germany; excellence as a motive in the Atlantic landscape; and the authority of the teacher, as a representative of state, in the East Asian system—a concept similar to that upheld in nineteenth-century Germany.

5.5 Differentiation in the Postsecondary System

As long as the university in Europe was a uniform institution (*Universitas*!) dedicated to the quest for and transmission of knowledge, the question of differentiation did not arise. This had already changed, however, by the end of the nineteenth century, when the market imperative of the Industrial Age required a highly skilled workforce with qualifications different from those which the classic university could provide. Nobody, however, expected this of the classic university. The technical universities and later engineering schools had another mission and existed alongside, not in opposition to, universities. The professional imperatives of modern society meanwhile created a growing need for ever-differentiated institutions in the tertiary sector, not just in the technical-industrial field. Thus, academic education for teachers emerged in the Weimar period and, over and beyond the national economy, a micro-economy at the level of enterprise. The penchant for specialization in the modern sciences greatly intensified both in and outside of Germany after 1945, regardless of the system. New disciplines, such as linguistics (not historical philology), emerged in response to the growing significance of language matters, as did hyphenated disciplines connecting aspects of one or two more subjects. This kind of differentiation took place, however, in one and the same type of university, namely the classic comprehensive university.

Alongside this, differentiation in the tertiary sector as a whole proceeded apace. The transformation of post-war engineering schools into technical universities at the beginning of the 1970s may be paradigmatic. Such processes of differentiation are due to various circumstances. On the one hand, extensive specialization should be taken into account; on the other hand, at least in Germany with its meritocratic system, the growing desire by a large portion of the population for an academic education, which, against the backdrop of the history of the German university, still had a good reputation many decades after the Second World War. In the 1970s, there was another push for differentiation when, in addition to the classic large institutions which had become mass universities and in part as a result of regional funding initiatives, smaller universities were founded. The newly-founded universities in the East Bavarian region from Bamberg to Passau or several similar institutions in the Rhine-Ruhr region can be seen as paradigmatic. While practical relevance or lack of such were used as criteria to differentiate between universities and universities of applied sciences, regional considerations were made in the establishment of new universities, especially as many of these institutions were intended to promote the willingness of regions close to 'old' or 'interregional' universities to encourage their students to study.

The third differentiation spurt was caused by the so-called "excellence competition," even if this was not the competition's initial intention. The competition for federal and, to a lesser extent, state funding for excellent grant applications in the area of graduate school programs, research clusters, and institutional strategies developed a catalyzing dynamic as small and medium-sized universities, due to their resources, had markedly fewer chances in this competition than the larger and more established ones.

This differentiation was an attempt to achieve an effect long extant in the Atlantic system. The differentiseation between research universities and all other institutions, particularly in the field of undergraduate study, had already resulted from the assignment of different roles, especially with regard to vocational education. This modus of differentiation had already left its trace in the East Asian system, as well—or rather, it met with a culture historically inclined towards differentiation. China, a country which is also growing in the tertiary sector, has created, with the help of its Netbig ranking, a benchmark, originally conceived for internal purposes and intended to clearly distinguish world class universities from the immense number of "normal" universities. The designation, since 1995, of roughly 100 universities by the Chinese Ministry of Education in the so-called "211 Project" and 39 universities in the "985 Project" (since 1998) laid the groundwork. The catalyzing effect of the excellence competition observed in Germany has, incidentally, found imitators not only within Europe (e.g., France and the Russian Federation) but in China and Japan, as well. Additionally, in China, as in Germany, the state's interregional/regional distinction is also at work. "Elite universities" can be found in the regions close to the coast but not on the border to Mongolia.

A modus of differentiation which applies within the continental European system, although primarily to Germany, is the distinction between university and non-university institutions. Organizations such as the Max Planck Society, the Helmholtz Association, the Leibniz Association, and Fraunhofer are powerful research organizations with comparatively far greater resources than the universities. Operatively speaking, they can best be compared with institutions in those countries that, like China or Russia under Soviet conditions, pursued research in large academies with close ties to the state. Such a system is not really known in the Atlantic concept. Here, state contracts and research projects, which in Germany are, moreover, realized in the specific research departments of ministries, serve as funding pillars of state as well as of private universities.

While in the already highly differentiated Atlantic system the question of differentiation no longer arises, this state of things is different from that in the Asian landscape. Here, and particularly in China, major differentiation between normal universities and world-class elite universities is being propagated, albeit for the sake of reputation. To this extent, there is a convergence with the continental European system, even if competition as a means of differentiation is inconceivable for the classic European system. Competition existed at best in the quest for knowledge, among scholars whose ideas naturally stood in implicit competition with one another. Making the best institutions visible did not require any grant applications. The competition was—as the prize essays or "grants" conferred by the ruling dynastic houses, especially in the eighteenth century, reveal—a competition of individuals.

In summary, we can conclude that there is a convergence, even if it arises from different motives, between today's continental European and East Asian systems with regard to the creation of significant differences between elite education and excellent research on the one hand and vocational training and perhaps something more like applied research and development on the other. To what extent this development may affect the Atlantic system remains to be seen.

5.6 University Funding

Even if the funding of universities does not count among the core categories of the three university concepts, it is still relevant as a condition for the realization of conceptual ideas. In this instance, system comparisons are extraordinarily difficult, even with reference to "official" OECD statistics, since the information often relies on self-evaluations and the question, for example, as to what a budget finances in the university sector differs significantly from system to system.

This can already be observed directly when we look at the share of gross domestic product for expenditures for the postsecondary sector. According to this, the USA spends, at 2.6% of GDP (in contrast to the OECD average of 1.6%), more on this system than all other countries in the world (OECD 2012). However, in the United States, the tertiary sector includes what in Germany is part of the secondary school system, i.e., the upper levels in the Gymnasia and parts of the state dual vocational training system. In the Atlantic system, circumstances are anything but similar. For example, in this system's motherland, Great Britain, the share of expenditures for the postsecondary sector is just 1.77% of GDP (OECD 2012). We therefore cannot speak of a uniform scope of university funding within the Atlantic system. Just as little can be said for funding sources. The United States' system depends primarily on the three pillars of state funding, especially through research contracts; endowments, i.e., interest revenue from the university's assets resulting from a marked donation practice; and tuition fee revenues. This means that the private financing of the system is paramount. Nonetheless, there are still differences between a simple community college and the large research universities. In Great Britain, the system is heading in a similar direction. Basic state resources constitute but roughly a third of the budget, tuition fees another third, and the remaining funding is derived from research resources, endowments, and other sources. The state's retreat from funding is a result of the world financial crisis, which hit universities in the United States, especially with regard to the depreciation of their endowments, particularly hard. A glance at the Brazilian system, which is equally influenced by the American one, reveals differences traceable to its strong Catholic character. There, for example, there are no tuition fees. With low rates of participation in education, the share of expenditures for the tertiary sector is, however, just 0.83% of GDP.

It is only in cultures of the East Asian system, which means the Chinese system, that expenditures, at 1.6%, are average, although there is an upward trend (OECD 2012).[1] Economic resources and private funding in the form of tuition fees are becoming more significant. In summary, we can conclude that in China, there is a noticeable trend towards university funding that is reminiscent of the system in the United States: tuition fees; industrial, state, and "excellence" research grants; and basic public financing of universities with marked differentiation. Due to the East Asian notion of duty, the circumstances in Japan with regard to the financing of universities via tuition fees is similar. The pillars of university funding have a ratio of 34.4 to 51.5 to 14.1% (basic state funding, tuition fees, and funding from the private economic sector). The share of GDP which goes towards funding is 1.5% (OECD 2012).[2] The highest in the East Asian landscape is the share of GDP in Korea, which is the same as in the USA, namely 2.6%. The funding pillars consist of the state (27.3%), tuition fees (47.1%), and other private resources, particularly from the economic sector (25.6%) (OECD 2012).[3]

To some extent, the continental European system differs from the two others significantly, particularly if we look at Germany. To be precise, there is just one pillar of university funding: the state. Tuition fees no longer play a noteworthy role and the share of research funding from private sources is 27%; endowments are virtu-

---

[1] Statistics for 2010.

[2] Ibid.

[3] Ibid.

ally unheard of (Statistisches Bundesamt 2012).[4] The OECD lists 1.3% of GDP for expenditures for university education (OECD 2012).[5] This fails to recognize, however, that in Germany, in contrast to all other countries, the greatest research investments cannot be attributed to university budgets but to external institutions. For these investments, Germany reserves almost 3% of its GDP. Of this, 1.97% is spent on research and development in the economic sector, 0.52% for research in universities, and 0.42% for research at external research institutions (Statistisches Bundesamt 2013).[6] In the other German-speaking countries, the proportions are, on the whole, comparable. This is especially true of France, where funding for the university system derives primarily from state sources. The relevant shares are 83.1% from the state and 16.9% from the private sector. Research in the universities is financed out of approximately 80% of the university budgets as determined by the state. Less than 5% of funding resources come from the private sector (Le ministére de l'Enseignement supérieur et de la Recherche 2013, p. 65).

To summarize, the system comparison allows us to conclude that, due to the respective state economic conditions and in part for historical reasons, the Atlantic and the East Asian postsecondary systems reveal the highest degree of convergence with regard to funding pillars. The funding of both systems is largely (two-thirds and more in the United States), and to a growing degree (in the East Asian system) non-public. This development has touched Europe, but not to the same extent. Many countries see the education system, and its postsecondary sector, as a social achievement which, consequently, must be publicly funded, and they give priority to the public interest in education.

It is only consistent that the admission hurdles in the continental European system created by tuition fees are not compensated for with scholarships, as is the case for 50% of the applicants in the United States. There is a discernible trend, however, towards founding private institutions in niche areas, particularly those in the economic sciences, which are (partially) funded by corporations and intended to facilitate the reliable recruitment of personnel. In Germany, the number of such small and even smaller private "universities," especially in the applied science sector, is now about 25% (Statistisches Bundesamt 2011).[7] This does not pose a challenge, however, to the public university system.

It will become more difficult to maintain the priority of public funding in the continental European system. This is especially true if, in Germany, the separation of external research and university research and teaching is not reversed. To ensure their future, the universities must have the resources which are largely invested by the federal government in external research institutions—from which the universities do not in any noteworthy way profit, with the exception of possible cooperation (the right to use external equipment in return for doctoral and habilitation projects for external scientists). Safeguarding the continental European system, which is

---

[4] Ibid.

[5] Ibid.

[6] 2.91% in 2011. https://www.destatis.de/DE/ZahlenFakten/GesellschaftStaat/BildungForschungKultur/ForschungEntwicklung/Tabellen/BIPBundeslaenderSektoren.html; Accessed 16 Dec 2014.

[7] Statistics for 2011.

essentially publicly funded, is only possible if the necessary resources are made available via earmarked tax hikes, if public budget priorities are reshuffled in favor of the university sector, and if, in the special case of Germany, the financing of the postsecondary sector by the federal government is made possible without restriction.

This is the requirement for safeguarding the core elements of the very substance of the continental European system and for countering tendencies which reduce the university system to financing just the natural and engineering sciences. The question of tuition fees also plays a central role. When tuition fees become the norm, the path towards a purely market-oriented university system is already mapped out, for whoever pays extensive tuition fees naturally expects a return on investment in the labor market. In this regard, circumstances in the other countries diverge as greatly as possible. For example, in Norway, the entire share of private funding is just 3% while in Japan, it is 51%, and in the USA it is almost 70%.

5.7 Individual Dynamics of the Three Post-Secondary Systems

What will happen if the trends towards system convergence and divergence, as sketched above, proceed from the previously passive systems or from an external, global perspective? The development is rather easy to extrapolate: the world university system which continues to develop thus would be tacitly and predominantly Atlantic. This means that an education market will effectively become an organizing category. Financing tendencies demonstrate this clearly: virtually all over the world, with (disappearing) opposition from the German-speaking and a few other continental European countries, the privatization of education—a public good—proceeds apace. A functioning postsecondary education system is increasingly seen, not as a public responsibility, but as a place where students brush up their resumes and interest groups from the production and service sectors contract research and development projects.

This will mean for the future that public interest in the postsecondary education system will also be quashed. These interests do not merely concern the chances of fair placement on the job market for as many citizens as possible and, in this sense, a functioning economy; they also affect the possibility for world knowledge and interpretation as well as the humanistic development of a world society via the cultivation of subsequent generations. This means that the theory of the university is changing so much that the academic system is transforming into a subsystem of the economic system. Alongside public interests, mid and long-term development prospects will have to be subordinated to the short-term cycles of knowledge production and business activity.

The revival of general education—now taking place due to manifold insights—by the introduction of elements of a liberal education into the otherwise specialized curricula of undergraduate studies offers no protection. In the Bologna variant of the tiered academic system, there is no place for liberal education, at least in the continental European landscape, because the process involves the simple conversion of the classic academic programs to the new system. For Germany, this is especially dire because the decision for an almost exclusively six-semester bachelor's program further limits the timeframe. More elemental, however, is the fundamental difference between liberal education and general education through academic study. "Liberal education" means, according to the understanding of study preferred in the Atlantic system, the accumulation of knowledge and the development of skills, as it does in specialized disciplines, but now it is simply being applied to a broad spectrum of subjects and a curricular canon. The transmission of canonical knowledge and skills does not, however, lead to the cultivation of authentic personality, but rather to a person capable of replicating cultural achievements without having had to work through them in the spirit of intellectual quest. We must therefore warn against simply exchanging the concept of general human cultivation for "liberal education" understood as the locus of canonical study.

We need to assume, with regard to university admissions, that there will be uncontrolled convergence. Even if, particularly in Germany, tuition fees do not come into question, a careless permissiveness in the founding of private universities charging considerable tuition fees may lead anew to the problem of fair access. The still-extant divergence between the continental European university understanding on the one hand and the two other systems on the other is worth defending with regard to university access.

This also applies to the concept of individual academic freedom for professors and students, which had historically been guaranteed in the continental European landscape. This must not be confused with the Atlantic understanding of university autonomy, since this in no way ensures the freedom of the individual. It is conceivable that in Germany, for example, the retreat of the state from the university's management does not yield greater freedom but that limitations on freedom originally imposed by the state would now be shifted to university administrators acting as agents of the state. Particularly if administrators act as university managers, then freedoms misunderstood as private privileges must seem like barriers to the implementation of state goals, which do not have to be identical with the public interest.

If, finally, we extrapolate upon probable developments in the world university system with regard to differentiation, then there will probably be a significant drive towards differentiation, as an organizational category to distinguish between above and below, in the continental European system, as well. More precisely, it is conceivable that the claim to freedom within university institutions could be reserved for world class universities, research universities, and universities of excellence by differentiating within the university system apparently according to function, but in fact hierarchically; for example, by distinguishing between research universities and vocational institutions or regional universities and "world universities," or between "excellent" and "normal." Since this kind of hierarchy-producing differentiation against the backdrop of fundamentally free access to a university of choice within Germany must lead, at the least, to demand for allegedly "top universities," such differentiations fit in the mid-term to cause the disappearance of those institutions deemed less illustrious. Conversely, top universities would lose their supposedly excellent character due to excessively high demand.

To summarize, we can conclude from these observations of developmental trends the world over that an "Atlanticization" is the most likely variant. Due to the economic status of numerous Asian countries, a primarily market-oriented conception of university education appears most appealing. In Europe, the question arises as to whether a system further weakened by the Bologna Process can or wants to withstand the growing market orientation of the postsecondary system.

References

Adorno, T. W. (1998). Theorie der Halbbildung (1959). In: (idem): Gesammelte *Schriften.* Band 8: *Soziologische Schriften.* Ed. by Rolf Tiedemann and Gretel Adorno (pp. 93–121). Darmstadt.

Altbach, P. G. (2011). The Past, Present and Future of the Research University. In P. G. Altbach & J. Salmi (Eds.), *The Road to Academic Excellence. The Making of World-Class Research Universities* (pp. 11–32). Washington, DC: World Bank Publications.

Henze, J. et al. (2013). Perspektiven der Entwicklungsdynamik im chinesischen Hochschulwesen. In M. F. Buck & M. Kabaum (Eds.), *Ideen und Realitäten von Universitäten* (pp. 53–81). Frankfurt a. M.: Peter Lang International Academic Publishers.

Kirby, W. C. (2008). On Chinese, European and American Universities. *Daedalus, 137*(3), 139–146.

Le ministére de l'Enseignement supérieur et de la Recherche. (2013). http://multimedia.enseignementsup-recherche.gouv.fr/evaluation_statistiques/etat_enseignement_sup-recherche/index.html#/66/. Accessed 16 Dec 2014.

Marginson, S. (2011). Higher Education in East Asia and Singapore: Rise of the Confucian Model. *Higher Education, 61,* 587–611.

Michler, I. (5 Jan 2013). Aus dem Studium in den Ruin. *Die Welt,* 21.

OECD. (2012). Education at a Glance 2012: OECD Indicators: United States. www.oecd.org/edu/eag.htm. Accessed 16 Dec 2014.

US Department of Education. (2012). "International strategy 2012–2016: Succeeding Globally Through International Education and Engagement".

Xin, C. (2004). Social Changes and the Revival of Liberal Education in China since the 1990s. *Asia Pacific Education Review, 5*(1), 1–13.

Chapter 6
Fair Chances in a World University System?

The risks of hands-off self-monitoring by the three university systems heeding the imperatives of globalization were recognized at a relatively early stage by international NGOs. For example, in 1998, under the aegis of UNESCO, there was a "World University Conference" resulting in a *World Declaration on Higher Education for the Twenty-First Century* (UNESCO 1998). Another conference of this kind entitled "The New Dynamics of Higher Education and Research" (UNESCO 2009) took place in 2009. Both conferences published papers which representatives of all three systems were able to support. This is no different with regard to the *Guidelines for an Institutional Code of Ethics in Higher Education* by the International Association of Universities dating from 2012 or the text *Affirming Academic Values in Internationalization of Higher Education* by the same organization, also from 2012, or the *Declaration of the Fifth Global University Summit,* again from 2012, and sundry other similar globally-intended ethics for the postsecondary sector (International Association of Universities 2012).

Acceptability to the representatives of all three world concepts is precisely the problem. The ability to agree stems from the fact that elements of all three systems are distilled and noted down as objectives at a generally highly abstract level. This compound leads, however, to a clash of individual goals and elements. The result of UNESCO's "World Conference in Higher Education" in 2009 is exemplary (UNESCO 2009). For example, if on the one hand it is decided that higher education should be the responsibility of governments but, on the other hand, there is a demand for autonomy, then this invariably leads to a discernible development (compare 4.7) whereby the state stays out of the management details while, however, potentially imposing, due to the responsibility invested in it, even more stringent restrictions on freedom upon university managements. Similarly, you cannot, in a single breath, insist upon "critical thinking" and "active citizenship" (UNESCO 2009, p. 2) as well as upon a closer link between the university and the economy—a link which would make it only logical to demand that goals which are in fact public be financed privately.

These kinds of texts (e.g., the resolution within the framework of the Bologna Process) often appear in ministries or in NGOs or in pieced-together, criteria-free world conferences whose participant lists do not seldom mystify experts. Indeed, such organizations and events are, in principle, in a position to help steer otherwise hands-off processes of globalization and to prevent unwelcome developments, but only if they enjoy sufficient legitimacy in their countries of origin; if they have the power to concretely implement and to propagate general ideas; and especially if—which cannot be the case—they unconditionally reject developments discernible in parts of the world university system. Since such conferences are places where interested representatives from the three basic systems of postsecondary education naturally want their positions to prevail, they cannot simply accept impartial analyses of developments in the globalization process. And anyway, there is no time for such analyses. Furthermore, it is unavoidable that such analyses are based on the respective viewpoints of the three systems of the tertiary sector.

Therefore, we must pose the question, for example, as to whether, from a German perspective—as the representative and "father" of the continental European system—developments such as those which Fostkett/Maringe predicted for 2025 should be promoted or tolerated:

1. A world-wide university hierarchy with a handful of top institutions;
2. A group of high-performance, internationally active universities within, however, the national university system and consisting of roughly 200 institutions;
3. A diverse group of universities whose spheres of activity are essentially national in scope;
4. Regional universities which do not conduct their own research (Foskett and Maringe 2010, p. 312 f.).

The authors predict that the institutions described in points 2–4 will have no choice but to fuse in order to become visible on a global scale (Foskett and Maringe 2010, p. 312 f.). This is precisely the form of differentiation, dictated by money, which we can expect with regard to the running of universities.

In accordance with the virtually inexorable dynamics of social systems we need to ask to what extent we can succeed in imposing some other medium than money—meaning to pay or not to pay—upon a future world university system. Asked more broadly, is there a realistic chance that the true/false paradigm characterizing academic pursuit can be revitalized?

This is conceivable for the research universities of the global type, but as well for those of the national and international type. To limit the true/false distinction to research universities, however, and to leave the other universities with a deficient mode of truth and falsity would be imprudent. Thus, we need, beyond the medium of money or the medium of truth, an endemic common thread in the postsecondary institutions around the world. There is no reason to reject the preservation or even emergence of national and regional peculiarities in such a globalization process provided there is baseline agreement.

This could be the case if it were recognized globally that, in addition to the challenges which need to be addressed by technology and the natural sciences, such as energy, the climate, etc. the societal challenge of dealing justly with one another in a global world also requires academic solutions. The solutions for these challenges cannot, however, be found in books and occasional papers but in the minds of educated personalities. There is no better principle for a global academic system than the commitment to the humanistic development of society and mankind as found in the East Asian idea of harmony and the continental European idea of education. This common thread is not suited to a narrow focus on research universities or elite institutions. It is valid for the entire postsecondary sector.

If we spell this out in the six fundamental categories used to compare the three systems of the tertiary sector, then the globalization of the fundamental convergence between the East Asian and the continental European understanding clearly means that the subordination of the academic system—indeed its integration into the economic system—must be ended without endangering the tertiary sector as a whole. The European examples of public funding show that this is possible. For the countries of the Atlantic system, this concept is no doubt tied to the necessity of opening the public purse in order to generate more money for the university system. The potential adversaries in this conflict have already been clearly named.

Education, as the responsibility of an academic institution, should not, however, be misunderstood solely as an opportunity for debate—as happened in the watering-down of the European legacy in the second half of the twentieth century—since education without knowledge and skills is useless. In the field of educational responsibilities, there is, therefore, possible convergence between the three systems if a connection is made between liberal education, which is characterized by knowledge and skills, and the classic East Asian academic idea, which is often erroneously characterized as exclusively repetitive; and if, based on skills and knowledge, education is effective for being acquired in the quest for knowledge in accordance with stringent methods of research and investigation. Convergence on a global scale is, therefore, possible through the medium of education in the continental European and liberal sense.

It is becoming patently clear that nobody may be excluded from this possibility. There is no theory of the university which would seriously exclude any of its own members. This has consequences for the question of university access and differentiation.

In German educational philosophy, the term Bildsamkeit (educability) denotes a person's fundamental capacity for learning. If there is, indeed, a fundamental capacity for learning, then it is impossible to justify exclusion from access to the academic system, which serves as the place of personality formation—neither with regard to the extent of an individual's claims to education nor against the backdrop of society's interests. For a society cannot afford to tolerate uneducated people to any considerable extent: knowledge and skills without education are simply dangerous. This means that access to higher education must be conceived as access to a system which is not institutionally differentiated. Institutions in which it is assumed that someone could be more or less educated, depending upon the extent of specialization, cannot be legitimated. For differentiation in the university system, this means that, at least in Germany, institutions cannot be differentiated according to levels, to wit: the more abstract, the higher the level of education; the more practical, the lower. Differentiation must be undertaken within, not between, institutions. This requires sufficient size and diversity as well as the inclusion of general core elements in programs which are conceived of as more practical in nature.

A developmental analysis of the three university systems shows clearly that there are different implications with regard to access and differentiation in the Atlantic and East Asian systems. The East Asian system differentiates, with regard to access, according to the ability to perform, the readiness to work hard, and the willingness of parents to pay; the latter plays a special role in the Atlantic system, in addition to the evaluation of admission qualifications. And, with regard to differentiation in the tertiary sector, inter-institutional rather than inner-institutional differentiation is discernible in even China and Japan. This generally applies, as well, to the Atlantic system, albeit in undergraduate education, that special but separate feature of research universities. One can by all means ask whether institutional convergence the world over is necessary if there are conversion regulations for degrees. An internally differentiated university system does not fundamentally possess less legitimacy than one differentiated inter-institutionally—on the contrary. Social differences are not documented and cemented simply on the basis of belonging to one or the other type of university. There is equally little necessity for regulating access to the university system globally. If a society committed to education, such as Germany's, does not differentiate when admitting to the university system but rather upon departure from this system—for example with regard to documenting achievements—then this system at least has a chance to tap into applicant reserves, a problem which may not arise in nations with other demographics. If these, however, have larger numbers of prospective students than they are able or willing to accept, then these countries have significant potential for conflict. To this extent, there is much to be said for globalizing the principle of the greatest possible access to the tertiary sector as applied, at least in part, in continental Europe.

The topic of academic freedom with regard to university autonomy, which needs to be seen in connection with the theory of the university, remains. Individual academic freedom as the freedom to teach, learn, and research has, with its constitutional status in Germany, manifested itself as far as possible. It also exists in various derivatives, however, throughout large parts of continental Europe. It is a global duty to establish this freedom all over the world. The East Asian system, particularly in China, is a long way from convergence in this respect. But even in the other countries, including those in the Atlantic world, we should not view this naively. Limitations on freedom—when choosing a research topic, for example—can simply occur due to lack of funding. There have been, moreover, scholastic tendencies, which have also emerged in Europe due, for example, to the Bologna Process, and there is the basic question of the constitutionality of study regulations for students and teaching regulations for faculty. As far as possible, the quest for truth must be guided academically and should not be utility-based. In all three systems, the broadest possible freedom requires the greatest of efforts if it is to be realized. This will depend upon a rejection of the suggestion that providing university autonomy sufficiently satisfies the need for freedom, because these have nothing to do one another and are, on the contrary, inversely proportional. We need both:

individual freedom and organizational autonomy, if the quest for truth is to follow from the necessary conditions.

However, the state's concern about the abuse of individual and institutional freedom, which prevents it from guaranteeing either, must be taken seriously. There is no question that abuse is possible, both in the harmless variation of faculty and student idleness which constitutes, in effect, misappropriation of public funds, and in the asocial or antisocial variant. If the state is to have that trust in academia which was formed in Prussia, than this trust needs to be justified. Owing to the massification of the higher education sector both with regard to the numbers of teachers and students, we can no longer blindly assume that freedom is being adequately exercised. The variant which ensures just a little rather than complete freedom is out of the question, since freedom is either total or non-existent.

All that remains, therefore, is the possibility of an ex post facto evaluation of academic activity in teaching and research—not by an inner-university quality task force but by a community of scholars. This was also the idea in the universities' founding hour at the beginning of the nineteenth century. Whether it was justified can only be attested to by the prominent examples of great scholars. Herein lies a chance, however, of inter-systemic communication with the aim of the greatest convergence. Academia devoid of critique is not academia; thus, facing criticism, even beyond the systems' boundaries, must go without saying. Incidentally, herein also lies a chance for convergence via global communication, which has long been underway. This example, however, also reveals that this globality may not be reduced to 200 research universities but that, against the backdrop of the need for criticism, it must go beyond this sphere of universities and embrace the entire system of postsecondary education. In doing so, the criterion will doubtlessly have to consist of evaluating the link between academic findings and truth. It is doubtful, however, whether universities today can limit themselves to this. The contractor of science and scholarship, the sovereign, has a right to know to what extent society, as well as individual life might change if the scientists and scholars he supports conduct research and teach as they do. In a society in which, like that at the beginning of the nineteenth century, so little was known, one could trust that research findings would somehow be vital. This is no longer clearly the case if scientists and scholars, for example, narcissistically tread the same thematic paths. To this extent, academic pursuit on a world scale must be liberated from one-sided interests. It will not, however, be entirely interest-free because objectives would uncontrollably slip in by back doors such as financing or reputation. Perhaps we should aim to speak of the autonomy of intention and concomitant social responsibility.

References

Foskett, N., & Maringe, F. (2010). The Internationalisation of Higher Education: A Prospective View. In F. Maringe & N. Foskett (Eds.), *Globalization and Internationalisation in Higher Education. Theoretical, Strategic and Management Perspectives* (pp. 305–317). London: Continuum International Publishing Group.

International Association of Universities. (2012). IAU-MCO Guidelines for an Institutional Code of Ethics in Higher Education. Resource Document. http://www.iau-aiu.net/content/new-iau-mco-guidelines-institutional-code-ethics-higher-education. Accessed 16 Dec 2014.

UNESCO. (1998). Welterklärung über Hochschulbildung für das 21. Jahrhundert: Ausblick und Handlungsperspektiven. Angenommen von der Welthochschulkonferenz "Hochschulbildung im 21. Jahrhundert: Ausblick und Handlungsperspektiven". 9. Oktober 1998. In UNESCO heute 1 (1999), 74–84.

UNESCO. (2009). World Conference on Higher Education: The New Dynamics of Higher Education and Research for Societal Change and Development (UNESCO, Paris, 5–8 July 2009. Communique 8 July 2009).

Chapter 7
Conclusion

Assuming that the emergence of a world university system is inevitable but should not be left to itself, the following premises and conclusions for and on the way to a world university system apply:

1. The assumption that globalization processes invariably lead straight to convergence and to an entropy of world elements is false.
2. Globalization processes proceed under the influence of technological, social, and cultural events and occurrences such that convergences may be filtered nationally, regionally, and locally, making new divergences by all means possible; this is also true for academia as a system—even if academic pursuit proceeds universally on the assumption that everything can be explained rationally and is amenable to influence.
3. With regard to teaching, the academic system is a fundamental aspect of an education system. Universities define themselves the world over as institutions primarily responsible for postsecondary education.
4. If universally developments of convergence can lead to national, regional, and local divergences, then national systems of postsecondary education as well as institutions of scientific research have a chance of avoiding the allegedly inevitable developments of convergence.
5. Nonetheless, there is a risk the world over of an academic neocolonialism, because competing social systems, dictated by their own rules of communication, tend to compel the collapse of the other systems or the subordination of these systems to other rules.
6. On a world scale, essentially three large system types of postsecondary education have remained: the continental European system, the Atlantic system, and the East Asian system. The system of South America, shaped by Catholicism, follows its own rules to only a limited extent and has already been "Atlanticized." This is not true of the fifth, Islamic-oriented system as manifest in the Al-Azhar educational system, the extent of which, however, is currently too limited both geographically and academically to play a deciding role globally.

7. The three basic systems of the postsecondary sector are currently competing for dominance. The decision about their future depends upon their answers to the common challenges facing the postsecondary sector the world over. These challenges can be divided into the following categories:
   - The theory of the university in connection with issues such as quality assurance, the relationship between basic and innovation research, and sustainability.
   - The idea of education with its attendant problems of a future academic curriculum and its standardization, the question of internationality, the problem of academic language, teaching methods, and—most recently—mass instruction via Internet (MOOCs).
   - Fair access to the postsecondary system of institutions seen as vocational training systems, in association with the massification problematic, the fairness question, the problem of diversity with regard to university requirements, demographic development, and student mobility.
   - Academic freedom and university autonomy as well as the related questions of democratization, governance, and university management.
   - The extent of differentiation in the higher education system with regard to both the local/universal and the general university/specialized university spectra.
   - University funding in connection with the problem of financial feasibility, financial sources, and, for example, the problem of intellectual property.
8. Presumably, the neocolonial imperative of market growth will lead to the disappearance of the three large systems because these will become, in the mid-term, features of the economic system.
9. Due to the absence of basic research—as a cornerstone of academia—such a development would lead in the mid-term to doubt about the very conditions of the market, which insists upon permanent innovation and new creativity, itself a component in the formation of personalities capable of judgment.
10. Under these conditions:
    - the theory of the university would become a theory of economic growth.
    - the idea of university education would be reduced to the demand for vocational training.
    - university access would become dependent upon private financial feasibility and testability.
    - academic freedom would be reduced to university autonomy, which represents an extension of state intervention in the university.
    - there would be greater inter-institutional differentiation in the university system and the unity of *universitas* would disappear.
    - university funding would essentially be privatized.
11. These processes would be the results of a dominant Atlantic university idea which ultimately goes back to a connection between the pedagogical realism of the eighteenth century and the pragmatism of the nineteenth.
12. Against this backdrop, the question needs to be asked as to what extent the continental European and the East Asian model have a decisive chance in the process of globalization.

Conclusion 49

13. This chance could exist if the continental European and the East Asian concepts succeed in renewing the validity of their historically much older convergences. These consist primarily in the facts that:
    - the obligations, and abuses, in the relationship between the individual and society are conceived as reciprocal. Society commits itself to providing the best educational opportunities, the individual responds to this offer with achievement and the willingness to work hard.
    - institutions of postsecondary education are not merely training institutions but comprehensive educational institutions which aim to enable the individual, on the basis of (self-)education through academia, to contribute to the further human development of society and mankind.
14. The remaining divergences concern:
    - the question of fair access, which only be achieved by the provision of sufficient resources and the eschewal of socially based selectivity.
    - the problem of academic freedom, which is the condition for knowledge both for the individual (cultivation of the person) and society. It cannot be replaced but only supplemented by institutional autonomy.
    - necessary differentiation in the university system which proceeds on an inner, not an inter-institutional basis.
15. The core of intervention from within the center of academia would need, therefore, to consist in a connection between traditional continental European and East Asian approaches, which aim for a balance between the individual and society.
16. At the same time, we cannot overlook the fact that personal rights granted to the individual in the continental European landscape in the field of postsecondary education fall short of or surpass, depending on your point of view, the duty-bound understanding of an individual's responsibilities towards society. This is similarly true for university access and university differentiation.
17. A conscious development of convergence cannot, however, proceed imperialistically, as it does in the Atlantic market model, on the strength of the status quo; rather, it must rely on prima facie dialogue between the continental European and the East Asian worlds.
18. To put it frankly, opposition to the Atlantic system is necessary for the countries of the continental European and East Asian traditions insofar as the laws of the market, education as a commodity, and basic research as a capital investment must not be allowed to gain further ground.
19. The recognizable counter movements within tertiary institutions in the Atlantic landscape, for example in the form of opposition to MOOCs or the revitalization of liberal education, must be grasped and exploited as opportunities for dialogue on convergence efforts between the Atlantic and the two historically older university concepts.

If we in Germany are prepared to think along these lines, then this must have consequences for possible conceptions of and plans for the German university sector. It means that, as exemplified by the category of university differentiation, the future cannot allow for further fragmentation of university institutions—of which there are now over 400 various types—but rather that we need to consider the emergence of larger, inner-German institutions, beyond the boundaries of university types, if only to put an end to the current political misinterpretation of inter-institutional differences.

In these critical developmental years of a world university system, prosaic official papers from global NGOs trying to satisfy everyone are less in order than activities within the universities, regions, and nations, and among the members of their institutions. These players, with their desires and their plans, must clearly understand that their activities are part of a global process in which opposition and dialogue must go hand in hand.

References

Adorno, T. W. (1998). Theorie der Halbbildung (1959). In: (idem): *Gesammelte Schriften*. Band 8: *Soziologische Schriften*. Ed. by Rolf Tiedemann and Gretel Adorno (pp. 93–121). Darmstadt.

Aktionsrat Bildung. (2008). Bildungsrisiken und–chancen im Globalisierungsprozess. Jahresgutachten 2008 des Aktionsrat Bildung. Published by vbw–Vereinigung der Bayerischen Wirtschaft e.V. Wiesbaden.

Al-Adeeb, A. M. A. (20 Dec 2013). Why Baghdad Needs an American University. *The Chronicle of Higher Education*, p.24f.

Altbach, P. G. (2011). The Past, Present, and Future of the Research University. In P. G. Altbach, J. Salmi (Hrsg.), *The Road to Academic Excellence. The Making of World-Class Research Universities* (pp. 11–32). Washington, DC: World Bank Publications.

American Council on Education. (2011). "Strength Through Global Leadership and Engagement. U.S. higher education in the 21st Century". Report of the Blue Ribbon Panel on Global Engagement. Washington, DC.

Blankertz, H. (1965). Problemgeschichtliche Vorbemerkungen zu den beiden Texten von Campe und Villaume. In: H. Blankertz (Hrsg.), *Bildung und Brauchbarkeit. Texte von Joachim Heinrich Campe und Peter Villaume zur Theorie utilitärer Erziehung* (pp. 7 ff.). Braunschweig: Westermann.

Derrida, J. (2001). *Die unbedingte Universität*. Frankfurt a. M.

Elias, N. (1969). *Über den Prozess der Zivilisation. Soziogenetische und psychogenetische Untersuchungen. Zweite, um eine Einleitung vermehrte Auflage. Zwei Bände*. Bern: Francke.

Elkana, Y., & Klöpper, H. (2012). *Die Universität im 21. Jahrhundert. Für eine neue Einheit von Lehre, Forschung und Gesellschaft*. Hamburg: Ed. Körber-Stiftung. (English by translator).

Frank, D. J., & Meyer, J. W. (2007). Worldwide Expansion and Change in the University. In G. Krücken, A. Kosmützky, & M. Torka (Eds.), *Towards a Multiversity? Universities Between Global Trends and National Traditions* (pp. 19–44). Bielefeld: Transcript.

Foskett, N., & Maringe, F. (2010). The Internationalization of Higher Education: A Prospective View. In F. Maringe, N. Foskett (Eds.), *Globalization and Internationalization in Higher Education. Theoretical, Strategic and Management Perspectives* (pp. 305–317). London: Continuum International Publishing Group.

Global University Summit. (2012). Declaration of the Fifth Global University Summit. April 29–May 1, 2012, Chicago, IL, USA. http://www.engagement.illinois.edu/globalsummit2012/declaration.html. Accessed 14 Nov 2013.

Henze, J. et al. (2013). Perspektiven der Entwicklungsdynamik im chinesischen Hochschulwesen. In M. F. Buck, M. Kabaum (Eds.), *Ideen und Realitäten von Universitäten* (pp. 53–81). Frankfurt a. M.: Peter Lang International Academic Publishers.

Humboldt, W. von. (1968). Theorie der Bildung des Menschen. In Hermann R. (Hrsg.), *Bildungsphilosophie*, (Vol. 2, pp. 56–60). Frankfurt a. M.
International Association of Universities. (2012a). IAU-MCO Guidelines for an Institutional Code of Ethics in Higher Education. Resource Document. http://www.iau-aiu.net/content/new-iau-mco-guidelines-institutional-code-ethics-higher-education. Accessed 16 Dec 2014.
International Association of Universities. (2012b). Affirming Academic Values in Internationalization of Higher Education. A Call for Action. http://www.iau-aiu.net/content/affirming-academic-values-internationalization-higher-education-call-action. Accessed 16 Dec 2014.
Kirby, W. C. (2008). On Chinese, European and American Universities. *Daedalus, 137*(3), 139–146.
Locke, J. (1897). *Gedanken über Erziehung, Translated, Notated, and with an Introduction by Ernst von Sallwürk.* Langensalza: Beyer.
Marginson, S. (2011). Higher Education in East Asia and Singapore: Rise of the Confucian Model. *Higher Education, 61,* 587–611.
Meyer, J., & Schofer, E. (2007). The University in Europe and the World: Twentieth Century Expansion. In G. Krücken et al. (Eds.), *Towards a Multiversity? Universities Between Global Trends and National Traditions* (pp. 45–62). Bielefeld: Transcript.
Meyer, J. et al. (1997). World Society and the Nation-State. *American Journal of Sociology, 103*(1), 144–181.
Michler, I. (5 Jan 2013). Aus dem Studium in den Ruin. *Die Welt,* 21.
OECD. (2012). Education at a Glance 2012: OECD Indicators: United States. www.oecd.org/edu/eag.htm. Accessed 16 Dec 2014.
UNESCO. (1998). Welterklärung über Hochschulbildung für das 21. Jahrhundert: Ausblick und Handlungsperspektiven. Angenommen von der Welthochschulkonferenz „Hochschulbildung im 21. Jahrhundert: Ausblick und Handlungsperspektiven". 9. Oktober 1998. In: UNESCO heute 1/1999, pp. 74–84.
UNESCO. (2009). World Conference on Higher Education: The New Dynamics of Higher Education and Research for Societal Change and Development (UNESCO, Paris, 5–8 July 2009. Communique 8 July 2009).
U.S. Department of Education. (2012). Succeeding Globally Through International Education and Engagement. U.S. Department of Education International Strategy 2012–2016. Washington DC.
Weiler, H. N. (2010). *Higher Education in Crisis. Is the American Model Becoming Obsolete?* Stanford.
Xin, C. (2004). Social Changes and the Revival of Liberal Education in China since the 1990s. *Asia Pacific Education Review, 5*(1), 1–13.

Printed by Printforce, the Netherlands